key accounts are different

'*A refreshingly practical route to creating a business partnership, and at the same time selling more to your key accounts.*'

'*A step by step method which could help any team selling into key accounts.*'

Richard A Humphreys
Chairman
NW Ayer Inc

key accounts are different

solution selling for key account managers

KEN LANGDON

PITMAN
PUBLISHING

PITMAN PUBLISHING
128 Long Acre, London WC2E 9AN

A Division of Pearson Professional Limited

© Pearson Professional Limited 1995

First published in Great Britain in 1995

British Library Cataloguing in Publication Data
A CIP catalogue record for this book can be obtained from the British Library

ISBN 0 273 61780 X

10 9 8 7 6 5 4 3 2 1

Typeset by Pantek Arts, Maidstone, Kent
Printed and bound in Great Britain by Bell & Bain Ltd, Glasgow

about the author

Ken Langdon is a graduate of Edinburgh University. He joined ICL in its sales and support organization and quickly became a salesman and then an account manager. For some years he was the sales manager of a key accounts team. In ICL he sold complex computer solutions to commercial and government institutions. Never a technocrat, he concentrated on what computers could do for ICL customers. Indeed it was mainly his customers who made him understand the importance of building logical and persuasive arguments for investing money.

After a year in the ICL training department, he decided, in his middle thirties, to get into a more entrepreneurial venture. He became a director and shareholder in Esprit Ltd. This gave him experience in the management of a fast growing small business. During his time with Esprit, he lectured widely in Europe, the US and Australia. The topics he covered included account management, solution selling, selling the automated office and business skills for non-financial managers.

He does not know who was more surprised, himself or his clients, when he found himself teaching selling techniques to major American computer companies. Customers he worked with included Hewlett Packard and Honeywell in the US, Prime and Digital. Indeed during the period with Esprit, he worked with most of the main suppliers of hardware and software.

For the last 10 years, he has been an independent consultant and trainer in his chosen subjects. He has helped an electricity company to produce business plans, and a telecommunications company to move from product into solution selling. His clients have included BT, Mercury and GPT.

He works from an office in his specially extended home with his partner in life and business, Penny Ariff.

For more information on carrying out any of the planning processes, contact the author at:

Kpl Associates
24 St Marks Road, Maidenhead, Berkshire SL6 6DE

Telephone: 01628 782193   Fax: 01628 771035

My friend and colleague John Wright created and experimented with many of the processes and techniques in this book. I gratefully acknowledge his huge contribution.

contents

introduction

Whether you are selling complex products or services involving high technology, or selling fast moving consumer goods (FMCG) in complex marketplaces facing change and competition, you will have some key accounts. Use this book to form a plan of how to manage these accounts for best results.

whether you like it or not, some accounts are key

When a new company starts with a new product, the product is the focus of the selling effort and the key element of the first sales campaigns. Success is very much tied up in whether you have invented the *better mousetrap* or not.

In technology terms, the product will first of all strike interest in the minds of technologists. They will examine it and decide if it has a place in the way that they do things currently.

The seller of the product is often its inventor. Inventors have an extraordinary ability to handle technical doubts and fears about their invention. After all it is not until they have thought all of these through themselves that they announce the product to the world.

It is probably up to the customer to find the applications to begin with, but the moment the first sale is made the situation changes. The first customer is immediately key to the success of the product and the company selling it.

The introduction of a new product in the FMCG marketplace gives a similar situation. This time the key account probably chooses itself by the similarity of how the two companies see the marketplace. It is also a function of volume. The key account is the one which will use up the production capacity which the selling company plans to utilize.

As time passes, key accounts in all circumstances need special attention. How we measure customer satisfaction, how we set our prices and discounts, who we speak to in the account itself tends to be different in the small percentage of the market which is of significant importance to the selling company.

You cannot calculate it mathematically, but it is something like the 80-20 rule – 80 per cent of our most important business is done with 20 per cent of our customers. Or potentially this will be the case.

key accounts need different processes

It has long been the case in high technology, that the tightness of the relationship between key accounts and the selling company has dictated that the selling company approaches these top accounts differently.

You can sum it up in a number of ways. The two companies know much more about each other. There is an openness in the relationship which reflects the fact that both companies gain from allowing the other to get very close to its plans and strategies.

As long as the selling company is adding value beyond the simple delivery of product, the customer will agree to sharing information and even plans with its supplier.

In FMCG, account management is proving more and more to hold the key to protecting and improving market share, while at the same time maintaining profitability.

Alliances are formed and last for very lengthy periods of time. The relationship is close and mutually dependent, but we must not go too far. In the end the selling team and the customer work for different companies. Their fundamental objectives and strategies may have lots in common, but there is never any doubt where their priorities lie.

We must expect openness and confidences in a working partnership, but we must not expect a customer with whom we are continuously negotiating business deals to reveal absolutely all. No more than we, the selling team, will to the customer.

What we need are processes which support the partnership in the long term, provide the customer with the business benefits of excellent products and services and the selling company with a profitable and predictable stream of sales.

solution selling

The difference in the approach to major sales campaigns in key accounts is mainly found in the involvement of the selling team with the customer's business. The team needs to understand the impact of the products under consideration on the actual financial results and image of the customer.

In high technology such a sales campaign would be an opportunity, probably in competition, to supply products and services which will enable the customer to do things differently. It may be a multi-million pound deal, or it may be a small project of great strategic importance to the customer.

In either case the selling company needs to understand enough about the customer's business to be able to couch the proposal in their terms and identify and agree the financial and other benefits of the project.

In FMCGs, the example may be to do with a particular promotion to which the selling company wishes the customer to apply resources of people and money. It may be using combinations of marketing information to extend markets and market share.

This type of business-oriented selling, we will call solution selling as opposed to product-based selling.

In the book we will look at how account managers gather the information they need to produce an effective solution selling campaign. We will look at how the selling team martials its resources to establish a persuasive business argument for the sale and sells it to the customer.

key account planning

Moving towards solution selling is the first mark which distinguishes the key account from the other. However, the real rewards from professional account management go beyond more customer-oriented sales campaigns.

Professional account management involves the creation and nurturing of a working partnership with a long-term perspective.

This raises big questions of investment in key accounts. Companies expect higher profitability and loyalty from key accounts. There are a number of processes required to effect that. These processes and concepts are at once straightforward to define and difficult to put in place practically.

We need to establish our objectives in considering the key account approach, and we need to get many people in the organization to buy into the practicality of the new processes.

Long-term plans take a while to gain momentum.

And we need time. Long-term plans take a while to gain momentum, and some companies are put off by the wait. But the power of the joint plan between the supplier and customer will produce such benefits in terms of revenue and profit, that the supplier must bite the bullet and give the team a chance to make it happen.

the plan's the thing

In the end an agreed approach to all aspects of customer care and selling emerges as the result of a plan.

This book is a practical guide to account management. It seeks to put the reality into phrases such as 'building a business partnership' a concept claimed by many companies but achieved by few.

We will try to explain in usable terms what goes into an account plan and the other forms and processes of account management. But be warned, if such processes are badly presented to the salespeople they will groan and complain that the bureaucracy of their masters is stifling their sales talent and leaving no time to get on with the selling.

This is the major paradox. We expect a key account to yield higher results than a normal territory. Yet we have to expend money and energy on matters which are not directly aimed at taking more orders and doing more business. Put another way, account management is where the argument between operating for the short term and striving to meet strategic objectives hits the front line troops.

We need a balance. If we are to get competitive advantage by dealing more comprehensively with key accounts we have to have a long-term plan. At the same time we have to satisfy the needs of first line sales managers whose bonus scheme and indeed whose essence is about achieving today's sales results and this year's target.

the book plan

The aspects of professional account management are covered in the following stages:

- The objectives of account management explains the general benefits of the approach and explains why key accounts are different.

- How a customer decides to spend investment money. This, if we are to have customer-oriented selling, describes the driving force behind an account manager's main sales campaigns.

- How one investment decision is made in the context of others and in the context of certain strategies which the customer has in place.

- The fundamentals of team planning. It is not possible for an account manager to form a plan and impose it on his or her team and company. The people responsible for the actions must take part in the planning process.

- Sales planning looks at the process of evaluating the situation and planning how to run a successful campaign.

- Account planning looks at the whole relationship between the two companies on a national and international basis.

- Organizing for professional account management suggests how the selling company needs to adjust to improve how it handles its key accounts.

EXAMPLE

Cases and examples

Based on my successes and failures as an account manager, I will illustrate all of the issues raised with actual situations taken from the *real* world.

I will also draw on the vast fund of cases and stories from the salespeople and managers I have worked with, whose results have given clear indications of how to do it and, of course, how not to do it.

Many of the examples are based on the selling of computer systems and telecommunications equipment. Others are concerned with selling FMCGs to large chains of retailers, which become key accounts by virtue of the huge volume of products which they move on a regular basis.

As I describe each of the processes and techniques involved, I will ask you to bridge the theory to your real world. If you follow this path, you will, by the time you reach the end of the book, have at least one key sales campaign plan in place. You will also have the outline of a professional account plan and a list of actions which you need to carry out to complete it.

1

key accounts are different

aims and objectives of account management

Why do we have to look at a large company as something different from a sales territory on 35 floors? Why do companies invest in their key accounts? Does the term "working partnership" have a real meaning outside the world of the business school and if so, how do we define it and how do we create it?

managing accounts for profit

A New York salesperson of fax machines had his territory or patch defined as the Empire State building. The territory was just the right size to ensure that he could get round all the prospects and serve his customers in a year. He put a machine under his arm, started at the top of the building in January and sold his way down to the ground floor by the following Christmas. Good, cost-effective selling with the minimum of travelling time.

> **If one corporation owns the whole block then access to line management can be more difficult.**

The question arises, does the salesperson look after the territory differently if instead of having a thousand individual customers, they had all belonged to the same corporation? Here are some of the key issues which make the situation totally different in the case of the large organization.

All separate companies	*A single corporation*
The salesperson can get to the decision-makers in each of the separate businesses. He's never far from the source of money and purchasing power.	Even if head office has delegated fax buying to the subsidiary companies and divisions, it can always undo that and draw back spending power to the centre.
The technical decision is made by the buyers in the individual offices, either the purchasing manager or the technical department if such a body exists.	It is often the case that head office decides technological strategy and imposes it on the divisions of the business. The situation is at its most difficult if the salesman is working on a division on floor 3, while his competitor is working on the head office technical managers on floor 34.
The line managers, that is the people responsible for making the revenues and profits of the business, are all accessible in a small discreet organization. They are financial, technical and user buyers (terms we will examine in the course of this book) all rolled into one.	If one corporation owns the whole block, then access to line management can be more difficult. The FMCG salesperson risks being confined to the buying department, or the computer salesperson to the technical department.
If the salesperson believes it to be a good thing to offer an incentive to one company, no other business will know about it or ask for the same treatment.	If he gives a concession to one division of an organization then other divisions will use that number as the starting point of the next negotiation.

WATCH OUT!

The left hand does know what the right hand is doing

This "arbitrage" effect becomes even more severe when we look at the more realistic case, that the large corporation is not just in the Empire State building, but all over the world.

An American computer manufacturer had a very profitable subsidiary in the UK. The subsidiary imported product from the US and sold it at the prevailing market price in the UK. For various reasons, to do with the price of petrol amongst others, there was a significant move in the dollar/sterling exchange rate.

At first the UK company was unaffected by the change, since the parent company set the transfer price which it charged the subsidiary on a quarterly basis. Then it was delighted by the change as the market price in the UK had not changed and they were buying cheaper from manufacturing.

Then it went nastily wrong. One of its global accounts discovered that it could buy the products cheaper in its US company and import them to the UK themselves. This cut out the UK subsidiary completely.

Not only that, but the global corporation realised that if it could do the deal for companies internal to the corporation why not for others? It started up a business bringing in computers from the US and selling at a considerable discount to the UK price.

From its position of comfort the UK subsidiary was now competing with its own products at a price disadvantage.

All separate companies	A single corporation
If something goes wrong with one of the machines he has sold, the grief is isolated. Whether it is the supplier's fault, for example, a Friday afternoon piece of hardware, or the customer's fault, for example poor training causing finger trouble, it will only impact on the individual company.	Bad news spreads like wildfire. The story of dissatisfaction will go round the corporation – causing at best delays in getting further orders while the problem is fixed, or at worst causing a review of the buying policy and the possible removal of the supplier from the permitted list. ▶

All separate companies	A single corporation
If someone in the smaller business buys something for no great reason, or a more expensive model than required because they like the look of it, that will be the end of the matter.	There are always auditors, financial and business process auditors. They will demand to know the return on investment of the product being bought and blow-by-blow reasons for choosing anything except the cheapest option.
Competitive pressures are present but limited in scope. If a competitor is doing well in one company the salesperson can afford to ignore the whole company. Just drop down a floor and start again.	Salespeople in this environment cannot ignore competitors wherever they are. Any subsidiary or division which is going down a particular buying route can eventually have an impact on other divisions or even the whole corporation.

The difference between these two scenarios is what we will call account management.

Even at this early stage in the book it is worth taking a moment to ensure that we recognize why sales teams concentrate their efforts on key accounts. In a nutshell, here are the objectives of account management.

● To gain marketshare.

● To improve profitability.

● To produce reference sites which will assist with other sales campaigns.

● To keep your product developers and marketing people up to date with what the market is looking for now and in the future.

● To improve the productivity of the sales and support resources.

● To get more predictable sales which are forecast in advance.

key accounts are different

selling the customer a solution

The Empire State building is of such a size that it is going to be difficult for the salesperson to understand the business benefits which his machines are giving to all the customers. They do not buy one if they do not need to send faxes. Beyond that it is not the job of the product seller to help the customer understand the differences which faxing is going to have on the bottom line of the business.

Solution selling to key accounts is different. The salesperson is working on the premise that a customer who understands what a product or service is actually achieving for the business is the sort of customer who buys more of that product or service. The aim of solution selling becomes not just to make profits for the selling company, but also to make profits for the buyer.

An account manager who was selling computer systems to a major telephone company struggled with this concept. He found it "intellectually dishonest" to take an objective which had to do with the health of the buying company as opposed to the profits of the selling company.

The customer called halt at one point, did an audit of all computer systems and discovered that he had more than enough and that some were simply not paying their way.

That same account manager was then on the defensive, trying to justify after the event purchases which the customer had made.

The objectives of solution selling are:

- **To make more sales by working with the customer to understand the return on investment offered by your products and services.**
- **To produce satisfied customers.**
- **To gain competitive edge by recognizing earlier than your competitors where the customer should invest next.**
- **To build customer loyalty by giving no reasons for them to look elsewhere.**

hunters and farmers

It is useful to divide the selling job into "hunting" or "farming". Hunting is about bringing in new customers, farming about increasing the amount and type of business you do with your existing customers. The skills are different and a major thought in people selection is to consider how much of each activity the job involves.

It is useful to divide the selling job into "hunting" or "farming".

For hunters, the main requirement is for persistence and the ability to take knocks. Theirs is the job which has them trying to get interviews with strangers who may not only be unaware of their need, but antagonistic to an unsolicited approach whether on the telephone or in person.

Hunters generally work quickly, have short attention spans and feel very dissatisfied if complications of product or decision-making processes intrude on their getting to the point of closing a sale. They are opportunists and in most cases need watching to make sure that the product being sold is suitable and will work to the promises made by the salesperson.

Some would say that it is the hunters who give salespeople a bad name. There is some truth in that, but they are also the people who make innovation possible and *en masse* bear a lot of responsibility for driving the dollar round in a growth economy.

The hunter is the salesperson who gets a high level of job satisfaction in getting a first order from a new customer. A seller of reprographics expressed it as "You actually have to start by getting yourself invited into the buyer's office. Then you must convince a probable sceptic that what you are offering has benefits over continuing with the people he or she has previously done business. Then you have to find a project, bid for it and win it. The great feeling is that you made it happen, unless you had made the first move and then followed through, that company would have remained loyal to its existing suppliers."

This is the typical conversation of a hunter. You will recognize some other phrases and sayings in their coffee break chat – "I thought I'd do one more door," "stitched him up in no time flat."

Every salesperson has to have some of the hunter attributes. A good farmer who hates or claims to be bad at new business selling may be too slow to go for the order or not sufficiently assertive to win against the competition. Once again we see the balance that is crucial for a professional account manager, between hustling to get things done and farming for the long term.

Farmers develop skills in long-term relationship building and deep knowledge of a customer's business. A professional sales team selling machine tools for example will build over the years a database of customer knowledge which the customer itself may envy. The benefits to management of professional farmers comes in terms of predictable orders, competitive intelligence, market changes and much more.

In FMCG this knowledge is equally important. The account manager needs to know the detail of the customer's strategy and interface to the consumer.

He or she then needs to know the results of market research and of course of actual sales. The more he or she knows about how the customers sell the product, the more able he or she is to make innovative proposals and achieve stretching sales targets.

An aiming point of professional account management is to be able to hold a joint planning session. The sales team works with the customer to build a plan for the next year in detail and three years in outline.

When this happens it is a sure sign that your company has truly created the "working partnership" and "added value". A lot of salespeople talk about these concepts, but misunderstand the difficulties and timescales involved in setting the partnership up and adding real value.

teams and virtual teams

A key attribute of the good account manager is the ability to use only charismatic power to motivate people to achieve their part in his/her plan.

As we will discuss in the section on organization in Chapter 13, best practice has the account manager responsible only for the performance of the company in an account. He or she is not responsible for the "pay and rations" of the salespeople and support people involved in the account.

The account manager for an advertising agency who looks after the Proctor and Gamble account worldwide might have over 100 people working in sales, support and creative roles. They all probably work for different line managers. This gives an idea of the complexity of implementing a plan without having direct control over the necessary resources.

Add that the account is live on five continents and 150 countries and the problem looks formidable. It is formidable, and the supervision and motivation of "virtual teams" needs attention both in terms of business processes, but also in terms of the skill involved in the management of people by leadership and motivation.

So far we have looked at the implementation teams working on the products and services being supplied. We need to take into account the senior management teams in both companies. Frequently the situation arises where a high achiever account manager has become a senior manager in the supplying firm.

This poses new problems. The customer's people will probably want to continue to deal with the person they know despite the fact they have moved into other roles. Account managers need diplomacy as well as business processes to deal with a situation which involves egos as well as business logic.

working partnerships

It is not possible to give a convincing description of a working partnership until we have discussed all the aspects of business and account planning which come within the remit of a professional account manager.

The key to it, however, is the concept of joint planning. For the moment therefore we will use the incomplete definition of a working partnership as one which *exists when the selling company is involved in the customer's planning processes, and when the customer is involved in the supplier's planning processes.*

key accounts *are* different

If we use professional account management techniques to handle key accounts, the results will improve. We will produce customer loyalty and lock-in. We will take follow-on orders with much less effort. We will produce reference sites to help us to sell to other companies, and we will clearly be seen to be making money for both companies.

We will produce customer loyalty and lock-in.

Having agreed that the Empire State building patch needs to be handled differently if it is composed of a single corporation, we can start to build the picture of the processes and skills which a business needs to farm and hunt profitably.

This book is as practical as you choose to make it. It contains action points at the end of each chapter. If you choose to do them, the action will help you to complete the process of sales campaign and account management for one of your company's key accounts.

As examples of the type of companies and people who may find these processes useful, I have invented three situations which we will visit from time to time throughout the book.

These businesses are based on real companies and are Dialcard, Universal Systems Integration and Nutrisnack. So that you can identify which case is most like your own here is an overview of the three companies.

DIALCARD The product which Dialcard sells is new technology. Developed in France it is a smart card with a difference. A smart card is similar to a credit card with a magnetic stripe, but it also has a microchip inside it which gives it an intelligence far greater than the credit card.

Dialcard adds another dimension to the smart card. Fitted with a battery it can in combination with the microchip offer some interesting applications.

A simple example is that the card can be used as an automatic dialler. You put it against the mouthpiece of a telephone and press on the appropriate place. This has the impact of sending the familiar tones of a telephone down the line and connects you to the number programmed into the card.

A major user in France is a car hire firm which gives out a Dialcard to its most loyal customers. They can use the card to dial and identify themselves from any telephone in office, hotel or even aeroplane.

Dialcard is new technology, and the skills required in the first place are those of the hunter, but a hunter with a difference. Dialcard will only make good profits when it sells the card in very large volumes. Dialcard needs a plan therefore which takes it into new prospects, gets the first pilot sales, but leaves a very secure base of achievement to ensure that the large sales follow.

The other attribute of Dialcard which will exercise its salespeople and account managers is that it is a developing product. It has a limited feature set at the start which will be added to as time goes by.

The biggest danger for a salesperson in this situation is that prospects will never be satisfied with what is available now, but will want to wait until Dialcard introduces further functionality.

Such a waiting game strategy may at first appear to suit the prospect but will inevitably lead to Dialcard cashflow problems. The company will have to spend on development but lacks a revenue stream until the customers are good and ready to order.

UNIVERSAL SYSTEMS INTEGRATION

Universal Systems Integration is, as its name suggests, a global systems integration company. Its parent company started life as a European state-owned monopoly, offering a telephone network to the people of its country. As has happened with a number of such companies, the Government privatized it. Given direct competition to deal with it had to change its methods and operations drastically to cope with this new situation.

It has, however, coped and is now an efficient network operator with satisfied customers and a wide range of services. Its next major push is to emphasize its already considerable overseas activities in order to achieve its objectives of becoming a major global player. It will do this by joint venture, acquisition and the growth of its international customers.

The systems integration business was built around the computer systems used by the telecommunications company, but is now concerned with many of the largest corporations in the world.

Account management is therefore as important to Universal Systems Integration as it is to Dialcard.

Incidentally, it is a common problem for a company such as Dialcard to have to present itself as a credible supplier to a company such as Universal Systems Integration. In relative terms Dialcard, which last year had net sales revenues of $200,000, has to prove itself to Worldcom, the parent company of Universal Systems Integration, which last year made profits of $3 billion.

NUTRISNACK

Nutrisnack differs from Dialcard in that it is already a household name and has a number of international brands which sell in huge volumes.

The company has many long-term relationships with key accounts which are themselves international retailers and wholesalers.

The products are a wide variety of snack foods. The US is the biggest consumer of snack foods, so we will study Nutrisnack in its American operation. We will also look at it in other parts of the world where Nutrisnack is growing its market share and the market.

By using a few examples, we will build an understanding of the activities of the Nutrisnack account team as it assists its key account Unistores to satisfy the demand for snack foods in its companies worldwide.

Nutrisnack's brand strategy is one of globalization. It considers the world a single market and wants its consumers to recognize the brand name no matter where they are in the world. This poses problems and opportunities for Unistore.

The Empire State building is a big patch whichever way you look at it, but it lacks the geographic spread which is part of today's account management challenge. So we will leave the Empire State hunter as he sells his way from top to bottom and concentrate on the wider dimensions of international commerce.

FAST TRACK

○ *Pick the key account you are going to consider and make sure you have the basic knowledge required to start the process of account management.*

○ *Do you know the businesses the company is in?*

○ *Do you know the structure of its subsidiaries and divisions?*

○ *Do you know some comparative size figures, for example annual sales revenues, number of employees and annual profits?*

2

meeting customer needs

how does a company decide what projects to invest in?

The driver of an account plan and a sales campaign has to be the customer. Until the sales team understands the political, financial and technical considerations which go into a buying decision, it cannot plan how to meet customer needs.

a *sensible* company's guide to capital investment

At any point in time a company is being offered by its managers and by outsiders many more ideas than it can afford to implement. There is constant pressure for money from product development managers, designers, information technology groups and others throughout the business.

This causes most companies to develop management processes for investment appraisal and project management. To understand this process we need to follow the *sensible* company's step-by-step guide to capital investment appraisal and implementation:

- Establish the objectives of the project within the company's business strategy.

- Involve the management and staff who will have their jobs changed as a result of the project.

- Agree the tactical business case including the cost justification.

- Establish implementation priorities and controls.

- Select the exact functionality.

- Select the necessary products and services and their suppliers.

- Implement the project and train the users.

- Evaluate the results and adapt the projects for improvement.

Each of the above contains lessons for the solution seller and account manager and requires some further explanation.

Taking the example of an information technology project first, how do these phases go? While we will assume a series of events, it should be remembered that in reality the implementation is much more complex and that many things are happening in parallel. Nevertheless it is useful to examine the process step by step.

ESTABLISH THE OBJECTIVES OF THE PROJECT

Many IT projects have as their starting point a strategic objective of the company. Indeed, if you look at the way banks have implemented their IT systems you will find that they have followed the rule of maintaining competitiveness by keeping abreast of new technology developments. From the seller's point of view this "me too" strategy is a fortuitous starting point.

It is likely, however, that the strategic reasons for buying will not be sufficient on their own, and managers will have to back them up with a solid business case. It is also important that IT implementations support the key business strategies such as product or marketing strategies. This is the first hurdle over which any proposal must jump.

Sometimes strategic considerations will easily transform into a business case and sometimes the link is more difficult. Consider these three statements from the annual report of the Burton Group plc in relation to its retail chain Dorothy Perkins:

1. **Building a powerful brand around a total fashion approach.**

2. **We increased profits through the tighter management of stock and a substantial reduction in markdowns.**

3. **Our supplier base is now very focused and works closely with us.**

If professional salespeople are going to form such a focused close partnership with this company, they must understand the reality behind these statements and build them into the business case for investment. In other words, sellers must connect the benefits of the products they are selling to these high-level policies.

The middle statement is the easiest to back up with a cost benefit case. It will therefore have powerful appeal to middle managers and the finance department. Senior management may regard any project's contribution to the first statement as being a key motivator.

INVOLVE THE MANAGEMENT AND STAFF

The only certainty about an IT implementation is that the jobs of some people are going to change. Most large organizations are getting better at managing such change. There are, however, still some, along with many smaller businesses, who handle this part of the process at best insufficiently and at worst with a lack of sensitivity. This imperils the success of the project.

EXAMPLE

Upsetting key people with technology

An example of lack of people involvement was the handling of a major electronic point of sale (EPOS) project by a large supermarket chain. The chain in question had some 200 sites in the UK and had an intention of introducing advanced EPOS, first in a pilot site and then throughout the group.

▶

The objectives were set:

- To reduce time at checkout and improve customer satisfaction.

- To improve stock control and shelf-stocking activity.

- To improve the productivity of checkout operators.

- To improve job satisfaction both in the front-of-store and back-of-store areas.

Given the volumes, margins and stock sensitivities of a supermarket, all the objectives were easy to build into a business case. Senior management recognized that the project would add many millions of pounds to the bottom line.

The IT people chose hardware and software and carried out training, albeit in the case of the pilot site just before the implementation. Engineers installed the equipment. It passed its acceptance tests and management looked forward to the results.

In fact the pilot was a disaster. Every single objective area produced a negative result. The queues were longer and shelf stocking actually got worse.

Customers' frustration took them to action which is the store manager's nightmare. They abandoned full trolleys near the checkouts. The process of replacing these items on the shelves is almost as expensive as throwing the whole lot away. Staff were so upset that key and long-serving people were leaving or threatening to do so.

What had gone wrong? The resulting post mortem drew the conclusion that it was the early stage of the project which had misfired. The people in the stores were unaware of what was happening although fully aware of the impending upheaval to their normal way of life.

> **It was the early stage of the project which had misfired.**

The implementation managers found a simple solution. During the build-up to each store installing advanced EPOS, local management arranged a series of activities guided by a package of material developed centrally.

Thus store managers received a box of materials. Instructions helped them to put posters up at appropriate times signalling the approach of the new technology. Store managers distributed newspapers with information on advanced EPOS including crosswords and competitions which added some interest.

By the time training was due staff were comfortable with the concept and the implementation proceeded smoothly. In the event, the number of people involved with training diminished and the simple process paid for itself time and time again. ○

Do not confuse this stage with training. It is helping the people involved to understand the benefits of the change to their company, their customers and themselves.

From an account management point of view the supermarket case throws up some interesting opportunities. If many companies ignore the familiarization stage in the implementation plan, could not an account manager gain competitive edge by helping the customer recognize the need for early warning systems?

AGREE THE TACTICAL BUSINESS CASE INCLUDING THE COST JUSTIFICATION

In almost all companies there is a standard method of making a business case and it is vital that the account manager knows what that process is.

How close the customer allows you to that process depends on your relationship, and how much value the customer believes you can add to the process.

WATCH OUT

Misunderstanding in the bottle factory

I was involved in the case of a bottle manufacturer who wanted to investigate the automation of the hot end of the bottle manufacturing line. In simple terms, machines manufacture the bottles in the hot end of the process. In manual systems people do the quality checks when the bottle reaches the cold end.

If you put automatic instrumentation into the hot end you can detect mishapes or other sub-quality product at an earlier stage in the process. Operators can make adjustments to the controls of temperature and pressure earlier, and the number of top quality bottles produced rises significantly.

Since you are improving the output of a process, the benefit goes straight through to the profit line. The return on investment is huge with the payback period as short as a year.

The bottle company consulted potential suppliers of equipment and invited them to tender. It did not invite them to take any part in the financial evaluation. The failure of the account manager to change this had a marked effect on the eventual profitability and quality of the deal.

A key issue in the tender was maintenance and reliability. The instruments went into a manufacturing process which was continuous.

▶

This meant that any failure of the instruments would cause the factory to cease production or produce a high number of reject products.

During the tender the suppliers strove to outdo each other with guaranteed call-out times, resident engineers and other means of satisfying the concerns of the customer. At the same time, of course, they were lowering the profitability of the deal, and raising the strain on maintenance engineering to perform to contract and customer expectation.

A winner emerged and the contract awarded. The business case which the customer prepared was an overwhelming one. It basically promised payback in six months and very large additions to the bottom line due to increased efficiency of the new process. The question subsequently arose: "Why did not the customer buy two systems to give fall-back reliability?" When asked, the technicians of the buying company agreed that the thought had crossed their minds but since the competing suppliers had not suggested it they thought they could save money.

When I asked the competing suppliers why they had not proposed the resilient system, they responded with a worry about cost. Because they did not understand the magnitude of the business case they decided to keep costs down by pushing the reliability and maintenance organization to their limits.

Incidentally, within a short period of the installation being live, the company bought a second system. This also had poor profitability for the supplier since the customer was able to claim, with some justification, an unsatisfactory solution to the problem

ESTABLISH IMPLEMENTATION PRIORITIES AND CONTROLS

During this step in the buying process, the sensible customer puts in the basics of project management. It is crucial at this stage to see the project in its entirety and plan the milestones which allow the business and technical mangers to control the implementation.

The key is to document every action and ensure that all the milestones have easy measurement. It is not enough to state "Test system for user acceptance." The salesperson must describe the tests in detail and agree the measures of user acceptance.

Here is a simple series of implementation controls. It concerns a proposal to use the Dialcard as a means of accessing a voice system. This gives the clients of a stockbroker instant information on the prices of stocks and shares. The customer can also request access to a dealer who can take and execute orders to buy or sell.

Fig 2.1

Dialcard A Stockbrokers Ltd

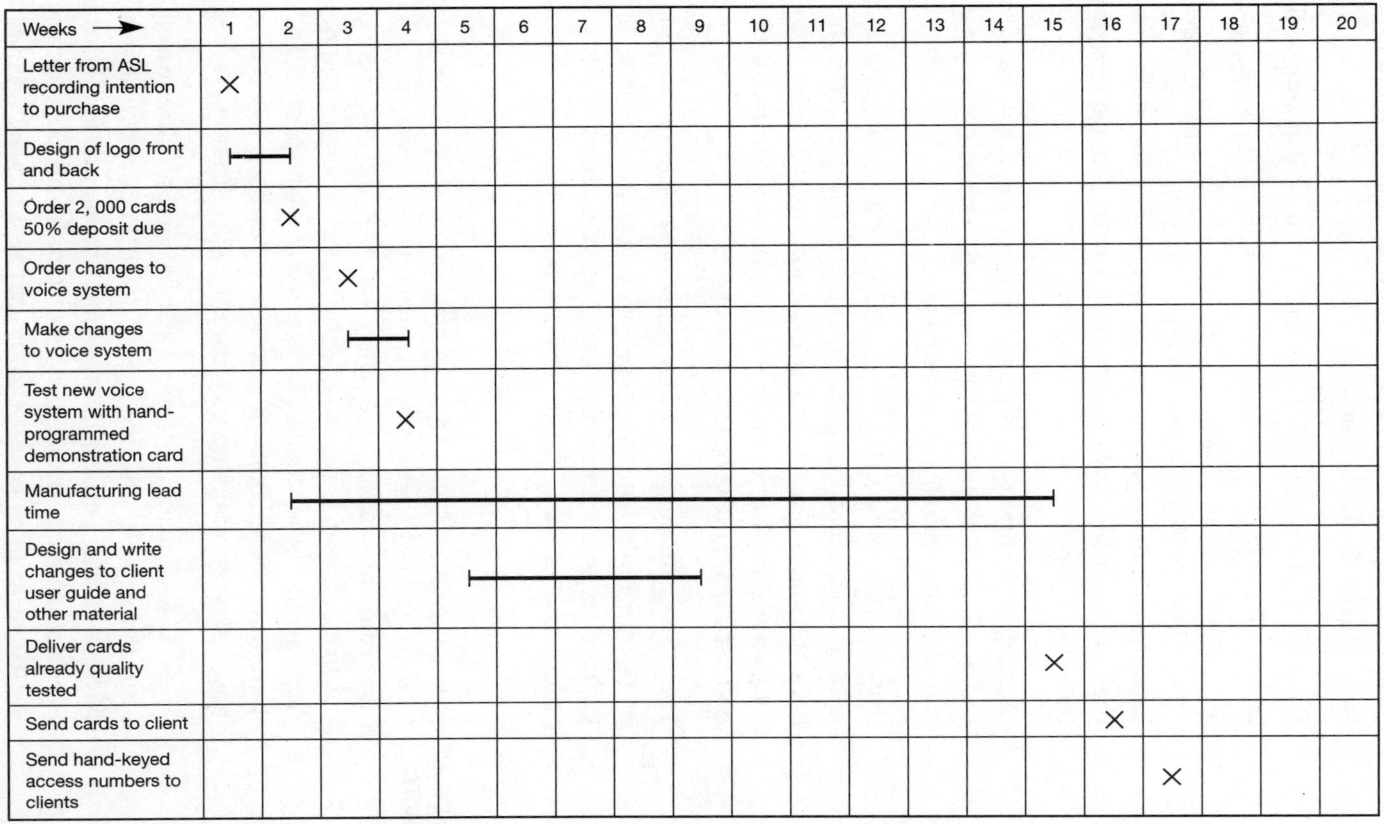

Weeks →	1	2	3	4	5	6	7	8	9	10	11	12	13	14	15	16	17	18	19	20
Letter from ASL recording intention to purchase	X																			
Design of logo front and back	⊢⊣	⊢⊣																		
Order 2, 000 cards 50% deposit due		X																		
Order changes to voice system			X																	
Make changes to voice system			⊢	⊣																
Test new voice system with hand-programmed demonstration card				X																
Manufacturing lead time		⊢													⊣					
Design and write changes to client user guide and other material					⊢				⊣											
Deliver cards already quality tested															X					
Send cards to client																X				
Send hand-keyed access numbers to clients																	X			

The job of a salesperson in this phase of the project plan is to suggest all the activities involved to ensure a successful implementation. Very frequently there are issues which the supplier is aware of which may be unknown to the customer.

From previous experience the supplier can anticipate some pitfalls and problems, and avoid unnecessary surprises. It can be tempting to duck some of these issues and leave customers unaware of something they will probably have to face and solve in the fullness of time.

> **Very frequently there are issues which the supplier is aware of which may be unknown to the customer.**

Once again competitive edge is available here. Someone else pointing out an additional factor unplanned by the potential customer, can damage the credibility of a competitor.

It is not possible to overstate the importance of getting this phase right and assisting the prospect to plan the project from the start, right through to successful completion. As we will see in the sales campaign planning chapter, no-one buys anything until they fully understand what the outcome will be.

There are also elements of an assumptive close in working with the prospect on the outline implementation plan. Notice how in the Dialcard example, the two events "Send letter of intent", and "Place order with 50% deposit" are given a date.

SELECT THE EXACT FUNCTIONALITY

This is the part of the project plan which the technical enthusiasts tend to enjoy. They survey the market for new technologies, study other implementations and talk to lots of suppliers. From these ideas and from a good knowledge of the future users of the new system, they produce the detailed functionality. Salespeople are also well aware of the work done at this time. They have two concerns: using time wisely and meeting the customer specification.

Firstly, is the customer using the salesperson's time wisely or is the customer wasting valuable selling time? When we deal with selling at different levels in campaign planning, we will need to look carefully at a problem in this area. We need to avoid the pitfall of two technicians, one the salesperson and the other the customer, spending lots of time looking at all the options now and in the future.

It's all very well demonstrating all the possibilities, but if the customer has no commitment to doing something at all the appropriate levels, then the salesperson is better off elsewhere.

The quick rise and slow fall of a banking prospect

An inexperienced Dialcard salesperson got a sign of interest from some business development managers in a large high street bank. The managers were very interested in the product and could see many ways in which they could use it in various activities.

Dialcard got some demonstration cards made up especially and tried out the card in many different situations to check that it would work for the bank's clients no matter where they were. They even took the time to go to Paddington Station to see if the card worked when being used on a payphone right next to an Inter-City train warming up for departure.

They found some snags and the Dialcard company put energy and effort into solving problems to make it possible for the bank to order the card for the first application.

The business development managers discovered a hitherto unknown department in the bank charged with checking the security, safety and reliability of credit and other similar cards. Supplier and interested customer went through the hoops expertly put in place by these quality auditors.

Unfortunately the salesperson had misunderstood where the customer was in this information technology buying process. They had started at "Select exact functionality" rather than "Set objectives and identify the application and project goals".

It is easy to be wise after the event but it is not up to the business development team to decide on new services. This is down to the line managers in the bank.

It fizzled out. The managers to whom the salesperson was talking became less enthusiastic about talking to him. They had probably found something else to chase. Everyone else he tried to address referred him back to the business development team. He had wasted his time and the bank was no longer a hot prospect.

The second point of concern for salespeople at this stage is to make sure that their products and services can do what the customer requires. From an understanding of their offerings and of the competitions they will try to ensure that any unique elements in their portfolio have a place in the customer requirement.

The end of this stage in the process is the production of a document which outlines the exact specification of the technology the prospect wants to buy. It is a familiar document for experienced salespeople. The prospect writes a matrix of the shopping list down the left hand side and boxes for all the competing supplier companies. He then places a tick or a cross depending on the presence or absence of a particular feature.

It is crucial for salespeople to involve themselves in this phase. They will be at a significant disadvantage during the tendering process if their competition has the ear of the prospect and they do not.

I well remember in times gone by, a UK manufacturer spelt the word for computer storage "disc", while its main American competitor spelt it "disk".

Account managers were always eager to see which spelling the prospect chose in the tender document, as this was an indication of where the customer's preference lay.

SELECT THE NECESSARY PRODUCTS AND SERVICES AND THEIR SUPPLIERS

Much of this book concerns this part of the process and the activities of an account manager. It is necessary first though to see what happens from a customer's point of view.

Senior management has a number of concerns. The key issue for them is that their managers choose the correct suppliers. This ensures that the project is successful, measured by "on time and within budget". They want the best deal possible, sometimes measured by "the cheapest", but in complex projects frequently described as "best value for money".

> **It is necessary first though to see what happens from a customer's point of view.**

Another issue is that their managers subject the project to their normal tendering procedures. They want to be sure that no-one brings unreasonable pressure on their technicians or buyers which would lead to them selecting a particular supplier and making a mistake.

Shareholders are very sensitive to any suggestion of sleaze or impropriety and senior managers look carefully at procedures with this in mind. Some would say that all of this neutralizes the best salesperson.

But, of course, when you buy the project you also buy the salesperson and the company he or she represents. Most people look for high standards of salesmanship and professionalism from companies with which they are about to do business.

The board looks at any capital investment project in terms of its relevance to the business and to its main strategies. "Is it hitting at the key issues we are facing and assisting with the implementation of our key strategies?" "Is it part of our general direction and will it remain so for the life of the project?"

Then the Board worries about organizational change. "Does the project demand difficult or uncomfortable changes in organization?"or "Will the project still be relevant and feasible after we have made other planned changes?" This last issue is made more significant if the buyers and implementation managers of the project are unaware of the impending change.

In the chapter on planning complex sales campaigns we will look in much more detail about drivers and restrainers in the buying process.

The lower levels of management and staff involved in the buying process have different angles and motivations. All of these can have relevance to the buying company and a great skill in salesmanship is to present the arguments to all the people involved in the way which suits their view.

Once again we will look closely at buying motivation later, but the following is one example of the different way managers look at things.

If a company improves its stock control system, it is likely to measure the success of the improvements by the resulting change in stock turnover. This is a ratio of stock held: sales turnover.

When selling to the accountants, the experienced salesperson will emphasize the reduction in the amount of stock held, since that is a relatively concrete outcome which the company can control.

The same argument expressed to sales directors will lead to despairing cries of "But we cannot give our customers what they want in the timescale they require it with the **current** levels of stock. Don't make it worse." The benefit of improved stock control for sales directors is in increased sales.

In actuality the benefits will be a mixture of the two, decreased stocks in some areas and more sales in others. Perhaps the mixture is the right way to sell to the managing director.

IMPLEMENT THE PROJECT AND TRAIN THE USERS During the implementation phase, the account manager has the overriding concern of ensuring that the supplying company achieves its commitments. He will ensure that it meets all its deadlines and produces complete customer satisfaction by living up to expectations.

People often say, and it is certainly true, that the job of the account manager is as much about selling internally as to customers. When companies make complex proposals, particularly ones which involve new technologies, there is always a risk that something will go wrong.

It is also frequently true that the account manager has during the sales campaign stretched the supplying company to make sure that the offering is competitive. This stretching process adds to the risk and it requires a dedicated account manager to keep his or her company up to the mark.

There are going to be conflicts of priorities at this time. An account manager has the responsibility to bring in new orders as well as to ensure customer satisfaction. During the implementation phase of a big project, account managers lose valuable selling time while they make sure that their company keeps its promises. As we will see later, however, customer satisfaction is crucial to successful account management.

The goal is to do business with the customer frequently and for ever. It is a waste of time to try to develop an account if there is any suggestion of dissatisfaction. You have to see it as building for the future.

The professional account manager also makes sure that the customer sees him or her as responsible for the performance of the supplying company.

I have often seen account managers with good relationships with their customers fall into the trap of blaming their company for any shortfalls in performance and not taking accountability themselves.

It is very important for the account manager to be present at significant moments in the life of the project.

This is a short-term attitude and in the extreme leads to a situation where the customer puts his arm round the account manager's shoulder. He then explains that while he has no problem with the salesperson, the supplying company is not up to it and he is going elsewhere.

It is very important for the account manager to be present at significant moments in the life of the project. Professionals make it a practice, for example, to be there when significant deliveries of products occur.

WATCH OUT!

There's no show without the product

I was involved in the delivery of a large computer to an old Victorian building. The only method of getting the machine in was to remove a part of the roof and lower it in by crane. The mobile crane had a journey of some 100 miles to get to the building. I had not done business with the crane company before and we had put a lot of effort into ensuring that it was there on time and did not let us down.

When it came to the day, the crane arrived absolutely on the dot and the engineers and others who were there for the installation were in their appointed places. The customer's IT director had come to watch the event as had I, the account manager. The only thing which failed to make it was the computer itself, which had unaccountably rescheduled itself for delivery the following day.

The embarrassment of sending the crane back along with the engineers and of course the IT director was bad enough. The only mitigating factor was that I was there to handle the feelings of the customer, reorganize all the activities and prepare for the actual delivery date. It was a very uncomfortable moment made slightly better by the knowledge that my absence would have resulted in an even worse situation.

There are of course good opportunities for the supplier in the training phase of the project. It is a chance to sell services and, if delivered professionally, the courses will give good feelings to the delegates.

The account manager has a responsibility to present all the necessary training to the customer. He or she must try to ensure that neither company takes any short cuts in what can be a crucial phase in a complex project. The lack of adequate training can be a major source of customer dissatisfaction.

EVALUATE THE RESULTS AND ADAPT THE PROJECTS FOR IMPROVEMENT

The sensible customer will take this issue very seriously. In most cases the technicians delivering a new system will liaise with the users to find out whether it is producing what they require. They will also agree the necessary improvements.

This iteration takes them back to the phase of the project "Select functionality". This type of evaluation is important, but the customer should not stop there. Equally important is to check that the project is producing the benefits agreed at the step which established the business case.

There is a prevalent attitude which says "We have spent the money and we are not going to go back to the old way, so why bother checking the return on investment?" There are dangers in this attitude. If managers believe that no audit will take place, they will tend to produce business cases which are much more optimistic than they would otherwise be. Similarly the skills in producing business cases will not develop unless management monitors the results of each project.

A number of large companies and Government institutions have developed large centralized systems. They have then made their user community use them as generalized systems. Finally they have tinkered with the functionality and failed to take a long cold look at the benefits and relevance of their centralized processes. This has led to inappropriate systems and user dissatisfaction, sometimes on a very big scale. Sorting out the resulting situation is very costly but if not undertaken will almost certainly cost the companies the loss of competitive edge.

A further reason why the account manager wants to assist the customer to audit cost justification is the need for reference sites. These are much more convincing if they can demonstrate business benefits as well as technical achievement.

This checking mechanism takes the customer back to the business case. The other check is of course on the strategic relevance of the project. The customer needs to ask the question "Is this still relevant?" "Could we make changes to improve the project's contribution to the overall direction of the business?"

conclusions

If the account manager is to be truly customer facing, he or she will be with the customer as he undertakes each stage in the process. It can be the definition of the difference between being a solution seller or just a seller.

A seller will become involved with the project only when invited by the prospect at the step "Select functionality" or even worse at the step "Select the necessary products and services and the suppliers of them".

The solution seller will involve himself from start to finish and may even instigate the whole idea by being the first person to identify the opportunity. This is easier to write down and say than it is to do. There are hazards to this sort of consultative selling:

- The customer may want to keep aspects of the project, eg return on investment, to himself.

- The customer may not see the requirement for carrying out each of the steps.

- It is time consuming.

- It requires the account manager to become versed in his or her customer's business and hold discussions on business topics which initially may not be part of a salesperson's comfort zone.

- The approach carries some risk, in that a customer going methodically through a process of this nature may come across reasons for not doing the project as well as reasons for doing it.

With all these hazards it is still the essence of professional account management to try to persuade a customer to identify the steps in capital investment evaluation. He wants to work closely with the customer in going through the process.

Prove that you can add value to your customers' professional plans.

FAST TRACK

- *Amend this step by step guide to fit the products and services which you sell.*

- *Take a project which has completed its implementation and try, as a post-hoc rationalization, to recognize what happened at each step.*

- *Take the result to the customer concerned, discuss it with them and try to sell them on the idea of involving you in the next project they are planning.*

As you carry out the action points use your experience and your company's to prove that you can add value to your customers' professional plans.

3

fitting one project into the context of the business

capital investment projects or new product innovations do not stand alone

---

Which customer strategies dictate the policy on capital investment? What impact does the supplier's products and services have on these strategies? How, therefore, does the pyramid of plans describe the account management process?

no project is an island

In Chapter 2 we described project implementation under the serial activities:

● Establish the objectives of the project within the company's business strategy.

● Involve the management and staff who will have their jobs changed as a result of the project.

● Agree the tactical business case including the cost justification.

● Establish implementation priorities and controls.

● Select the exact functionality.

● Select the necessary products and services and the suppliers of them.

● Implement the project and train the users.

● Evaluate the results and adapt the projects for improvement.

But this is not the whole story. Whether the project is at head office or subsidiary level it will have drivers which are to do with the company's goals and with the company's strategies.

FAST TRACK

○ *Take a look at the following pyramid of plans of an electricity company. With your products and services in mind, consider which business goals and strategies would have the most impact on your account strategy.*

BUSINESS GOALS AND OBJECTIVES

A buying company has a pyramid of plans. The goals and aspirations of one part of the business impact significantly on the plans of the next level down.

An electricity company has the following business structure:

Fig 3.1

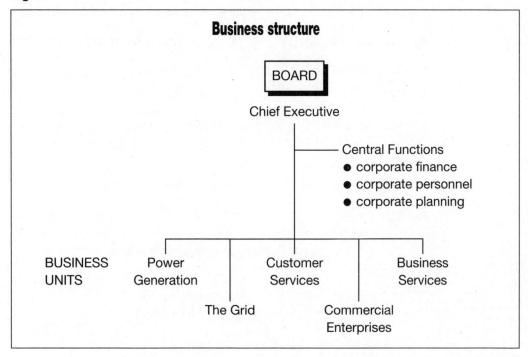

Business structure

BOARD

Chief Executive

Central Functions
- corporate finance
- corporate personnel
- corporate planning

BUSINESS UNITS

Power Generation

Customer Services

Business Services

The Grid

Commercial Enterprises

The three business units which produce and deliver the products are Power Generation, The Grid and Customer Services. It is useful to call the managers in these units the "line management". The other businesses are support business units or have a plan to sell other types of non-core services outside the group.

The pyramid of plans will thus start from a corporate plan. This plan will be a significant part of the business units' business environment.

Take the example of the Power Generating business unit. From the corporate plan will emerge key goals such as the price of a unit to a customer, the profitability of the whole organization, personnel goals in global terms (number of people to be employed), safety levels, environmental issues and a host of other aspirations.

When the Generating business unit does its plan, all of these considerations will have their impact. Some of them will offer no problems to the business unit. It may wish to question others or seek some modification if an issue is likely to prevent the business unit from achieving its goals.

When the head office of the Power Generation business unit made its plan it decided to produce goals in six areas:

- Plant and machinery.
- Environment.
- Safety.
- Industrial relations.
- Organization.
- Finance.

These in turn will impact the next level of planning which is each individual power station. This trickles down through the management structure as follows:

Fig 3.2

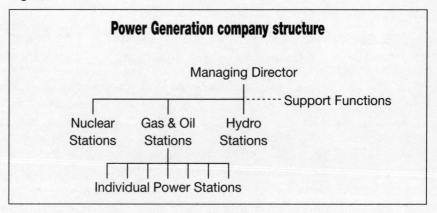

Power Generation company structure

Managing Director

Support Functions

Nuclear Stations   Gas & Oil Stations   Hydro Stations

Individual Power Stations

The professional account manager wants to know the strategy at each level of those goals which impact on purchasing decisions in his or her area.

"If I sell items of plant to hydro station managers I will certainly want to understand the plant strategy at all levels. What is the life cycle planning method? What levels of availability will station managers and senior managers expect?"

There may also be some other strategies which will have a real though less direct impact on the electricity company's buying plans. Issues of staffing and industrial relations, some of which are at corporate level, may present difficulties in introducing new technology. The professional account manager will pay attention to these issues even though at first sight they seem outside his or her sphere of influence.

In some cases, the account manager will change the presentation of the new ideas to reflect employee concerns. In extreme cases, the account manager will understand that there is little chance of the project going ahead until the management has solved the industrial relations issues. A withdrawal at that stage could save a lot of time and effort on the part of the supplier. Let us take two examples, Universal Systems Integration and Nutrisnack.

> **In some cases the account manager will change the presentation of the new ideas to reflect employee concerns.**

Universal Systems Integration has an electricity company as a key account. It has already bid for and won contracts to install new computer systems in the generating side of the business and wishes to introduce a new maintenance system to the distribution business unit.

Using its contacts with senior management, it understands the main goals and strategies which it has handed down to the customer service business unit. It then has to discover how the business unit interprets and implements those strategies in its business plan.

Universal Systems Integration will see the issues which impact on the buying process significantly as follows:

1. **Overall company goals for one to five years.**

2. **Distribution business goals for one to five years.**

3. **Plant and machinery strategy.**

4. **Information technology strategy.**

The amount of detail which the account manager will require will depend on the potential impact on any proposal he may make. In the case of plant strategy, the focus will be on the issues of maintenance and it will probably be possible to state them briefly and simply. In the case of the information strategy he may well need to understand it much more deeply. The picture for item 4 changes to this:

Management strategy. Who owns the information technology assets? What degree of centralization is there? What does management require in terms of standards and security? There are other considerations in this strategy all of which Universal needs to understand.

Applications strategy. What are the requirements for information? Who allocates resources and what are the current priorities? How does the company plan its projects, etc?

Technology strategy. What are the strategies for data, communications, computer distribution software and suppliers?

The account manager who is close to all of this will have enormous competitive edge over people who are more cursory in their information gathering.

All four of these strategies drive and influence each stage of the project plan with which we are already familiar from Chapter 2. We can now agree that the job of the solution seller is to work with the customer through each step of the project. The job of the account manager includes taking into account all the other elements of business plans and strategies, in this case from 1 to 4.

Exactly the same concept occurs in the FMCG field. Nutrisnack has a key account called Unistore. The account manager has developed contacts high and wide in the organization so as to be very aware of the various strategies which impact on the buying processes.

In this case, the key issue is how the channel, Unistore, plans to react with the consumer. The account manager makes sure that there is a fit between the Unistore company and Nutrisnack. From detailed knowledge of Unistore's plans for promotions, advertising, new product offerings and other issues, the account manager is able to do his own internal and external selling to mould the overlaps of the two companies' plans.

Notice however, that the Unistore account manager cannot compromise the Nutrisnack strategy. However Unistore tackles the interface with the consumer, Nutrisnack has an image which is universal. It is brand differentiation which enables Nutrisnack to compete in the world of own-branded products, and Unistore must take no actions which alters or compromises that image.

Once again, in professional account management there has to be good chemistry between the supplier and the customer. In extreme cases, a Nutrisnack account manager will have to recognize irreconcilable differences either in the whole company philosophy or in particular categories of product.

The long-term relationship with Unistore is as open as it is commercially possible to achieve. If the two companies are to assist each other in sales volume and profitability, they must share in some detail their operating and strategic plans.

> **They must share in some detail their operating and strategic plans.**

EXAMPLE

Adding value internationally

An FMCG supplier to a UK retailer gained competitive edge by using knowledge of a new market which the retailer wanted to reach. The account manager had a good enough contact level to be aware of the international aspirations of his account.

The retailer had decided to tackle Hungary for various reasons. The account manager investigated with his international division what their activities were in Hungary. He discovered that there was a distribution channel there and spoke with the people involved.

His colleagues in Hungary talked about the significant differences in doing business in that country. There are different standards and ways of concluding contracts. The supplier was able to introduce his customer to some key people in the country. They were also able to assist with educating management in the ways of the Hungarian business world.

The UK account manager put time and effort into this project. He did this, not because it gave rise to extra volume in the UK, but because it was a good example of the working partnership adding value to the retailer's business. ○

In the next chapter we will look at the pyramid of plans from the supplier's point of view. For the moment, finish the action proposed at the start of this chapter.

FAST TRACK

○ *List the plans and strategies of your account which you will need to understand to carry out the account management side of your job.*

4

the fundamentals of preparing practical plans

making the team planning process work

Who needs to be involved in a planning event? What are the different types of plan the account manager needs to undertake and understand? How long does it take and is it a cost effective use of resources? What are the guidelines for running a successful event and how do you judge the quality of the resulting plan?

the business planning process

Any organization needs to create plans which are accepted by the people involved in their implementation. Plans are required at all levels in the organization and should cover strategic and tactical issues. They need to include data from the broadest vision statement to the detailed matrix of numbers on which the managers at all levels are going to brief shareholders and monitor the performance of the business.

The account manager is concerned with the business plans of the selling company and also with the plans of the key account. Account managers of large worldwide accounts will find themselves spending much of their time in planning meetings. They will assist the various sales and support people round the world to produce a coherent set of activities to maximize sales and profits and maintain a long-term relationship with the key account.

Without doubt the account manager will require plans of three types:

- Key sales campaign plans.

- Key account plans.

- The sales operating plan.

The account manager may also be involved with the customer's planning processes and activities concerned with building teamwork. To the list of definites we can add the possibles "business planning" and "team building".

It is useful for the account manager to recognize some basics about planning which are always relevant whatever plan he or she is dealing with. The basics are:

- The aims of a planning process.

- An outline of the planning process.

- The pyramid of account management plans.

- The timing of the formal process.

- Who should be there?

- How long does it take?

- Setting up the planning environment.

- Using a facilitator in the planning process.

The French word for a map is "le Plan". In many ways that is the short-est explanation for what a good plan is. It is a map for how a team is going to get where it wants to be.

The problems are: "How do we produce account plans and campaign plans which will be accepted by all the people concerned? How do we make sure that the plan is used by the account manager as an essential road map to success? What sort of plans allow man-agement to control their part of the busi-ness, and senior management to monitor the long-term and operational achieve-ments of the whole company?"

> **Make sure that the plan is used by the account manager as an essential road map to success.**

The answer has to be to adopt a planning process which properly tackles "Implementability". The process, for both key account and campaign plans, must:

- Be a team approach where everyone involved in the implemen-tation of the plan is also involved in its conception.

- Be an essential tool in managing the account or campaign. It has to form the key control document and people must want to use it in everyday life.

- Be a live, changing document reflecting a lively, changing work-ing environment.

- Be a mechanism by which individuals accept accountability for the carrying out of actions and achievement of goals.

The easy answer to the question "When should we use a formal plan-ning process?" is "Whenever you need to". It is impossible to predict in what circumstances a formal planning process would be appropri-ate. Account managers who understand how the process works are likely to get better at judging when it is appropriate to use the disci-plines of such a session.

In the chapter on organization I will make some general suggestions. DO use a recognized process:

- When a new account team is being formed.

- When a campaign team or virtual team has been created.

- Regularly as a reviewing or creative process, e.g:

  - Annual review – two days off-site

  - Monthly Review – one day on-site

  - As required for a major issue one or two days on or off-site.

- When a number of team members have changed, in order to get the creativity and buy-in of the new people.

- As a team building process.

NB. A facilitator may add value to any of the above uses of the process.

DO NOT use the process:

- When it is a sledge-hammer to crack a nut, ie when a meeting could be held, discussion take place and decisions made.

- When the administrative burden is higher than the value of the planning session.

- To expose weak members of a team to his or her colleagues.

AN OUTLINE OF THE PLANNING PROCESS

I prefer to call the formal session which produces a plan a creative planning process. Whether you are planning a key account or a sales campaign you will eventually have to gain the agreement of management that the goals in the plan are appropriate and that the resources required are reasonable and available.

To begin with the team needs to take a creative approach to ensure that the plan is not simply born from "same as last year plus ten per cent" and re-examines some issues which may have been seen as givens. The first three steps in the creative planning process are:

- *Analyze* the current situation (commonly called environmental analysis).

- *Set* the objectives which the team decides are the most stretching which can be achieved given the current position.

- *Agree* the actions required to achieve those objectives.

For the different types of plan there are different techniques in each of these steps but for now we will concern ourselves with the relative amounts of time each part of the process occupies.

Experience has shown that the relative amounts of time are as follows. If it takes one unit of time (eg a day or an hour) to set the goals, you will probably find that it takes three times that to agree the current situation, ie to do the environmental analysis. This relative timing is represented in Figure 4.1 which demonstrates diagramatically the relative amounts of time required by each step of the planning process.

Fig 4.1

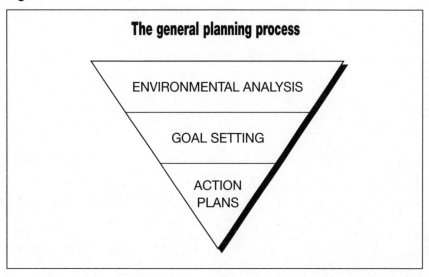

In some companies where planning has been stitched into the culture of the organization, the upside-down triangle has become as meaningful a symbol as π.

In a moment we will see how account plans are normally a pyramid of plans, covering different subsidiaries of the key account or different geographies or whatever other organization makes sense. This pyramid of plans is most easily represented by the upside-down triangle (I use the symbol here and throughout the book, as it reminds us that team planning is a general process).

> **Account plans are normally a pyramid of plans.**

The next two steps in the process are:

● *Create the resource plan*. From the goals and actions the team has created, it should be straightforward to produce a resource plan. This will include the detail of the skills required, when they are required and how long they will be needed. Where possible the team should include actual names of the individuals they would like to involve.

● *Review the plan with management* to get a decision on whether or not the resources will be made available for implementing the plan. Since the account manager does not have direct responsibility for the resources required by the plan, there needs to be a moment when the team is told that they will have the ability to carry out the plan.

To the diagram of the planning process we can add the resource plan and a decision box to reflect the point at which management allocates resources to the plan. See Figure 4.2.

Fig 4.2

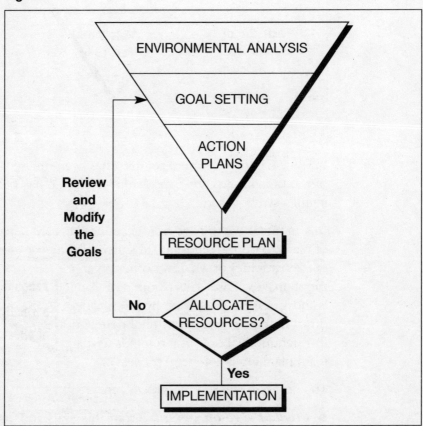

After one or more iterations of the resource loop, the team is in a position to implement the plan. Nothing stays the same for long however, and the time will come quite quickly when the team needs to revisit the plan together.

The account manager is responsible for the upkeep of the plan and will have to decide when such reviews are necessary. In the chapter on organization, I have made some suggestions based on the experience of many teams. It is a very personal thing though in the end, and I prefer to let the account managers work out their own routine rather than impose a schedule on them.

Figure 4.3 adds review to complete the individual planning process.

Fig 4.3

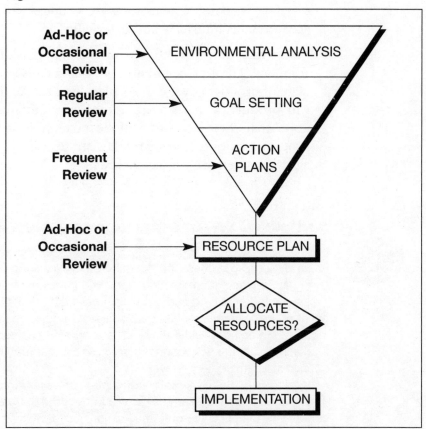

I will describe and give examples of account planning and sales campaign planning in the appropriate chapter. For the moment we have seen the general creative planning process.

THE PYRAMID OF ACCOUNT MANAGEMENT PLANS

But, of course, any plan depends to a greater or lesser extent on input from other plans. Let us take the key account plan as the central driver of an account manager's activities, and add the internal plans which will impact on that.

- A key driver will be the operating plan of the supplying company. This will contain, amongst other things, details of the sales and profit aspirations which management has for the key account. It will also contain key strategies and policies which the account plan must accept and operate under. An account plan must not compromise the integrity of the company's business plans. Account managers must never forget the knock-on effect of making concessions or changes to policy. A key account talks internally and externally.

- Another key driver will be the marketing plans of the supplying company. Through segmentation, market research and knowledge of product development plans, the marketing department will produce a marketing strategy. Account managers always hope that their account will be taken into account in that process, but once the marketing strategy is set account managers must live with it (see below).

TRICKS OF THE TRADE

Avoid having as many marketing strategies as you have key accounts

I spent some time helping a computer major to implement this creative planning process into its culture. There was to start with a large gap between its marketing plans and its account plans.

It was not difficult to find out why. I attended the annual planning event of the team looking after a significant account in the aerospace industry. On being asked if the team had seen the aerospace sector marketing plan, the account manager said she had but it had not contained anything very relevant.

I got a copy of the marketing document and went through some of the key points. The team ticked a number of the strategies and activities in the plan. To some they simply said that it was wrong, or that it may be right for the rest of the market but it was not right for their customer.

▶

When I spoke to the marketing director and his people, they were understandably angry with the attitude of the team. I asked to spend some time with the team in the account planning session. To begin with the atmosphere was very unfriendly.

Then the marketing people saw an example of a difference of approach which could be resolved by a change to the marketing plan which did not give them a problem. Then the team did the same thing, made a minor modification which helped the compatibility of the two plans.

They were now ready at least to discuss the main issues of serious contention. They made a lot of progress, but could not agree on everything without further reference to the customer. They planned a joint meeting with the customer.

At that meeting they discovered that the customer, too, could make minor changes which added to the compatibility, and so it went on. In the end there were still some exceptions, but the key account team and marketing were very much nearer together.

The company resolved to have a marketing representative at as many of the key account planning events as possible. The account teams for their part agreed to give marketing people more access to their customers.

- To the list of influencing plans we could add many more. Perhaps product plans or product development plans will be a significant factor. In FMCG the IT plan of the supplying company could have an impact on the market information part of the account plan.

In terms of adding to the diagram of the pyramid of plans, I will add the two most likely influencers (see Figure 4.4). The feedback loops among the plans will help to mature and improve all types of plans in the organization.

I will illustrate this feedback loop in the context of other sub-account plans which deal with other parts of the customer.

- *Geographic plans.* In an international account there will probably be sub-account plans for each significant territory or country. In a UK key account where the head office of the customer is in London, the US key account plan must interface with the UK account plan. It is a bottom-up and top-down approach. The sub-account manager will probably attend the main planning meetings of the whole team and the account manager should certainly attend the planning meetings of the US team.

Fig 4.4

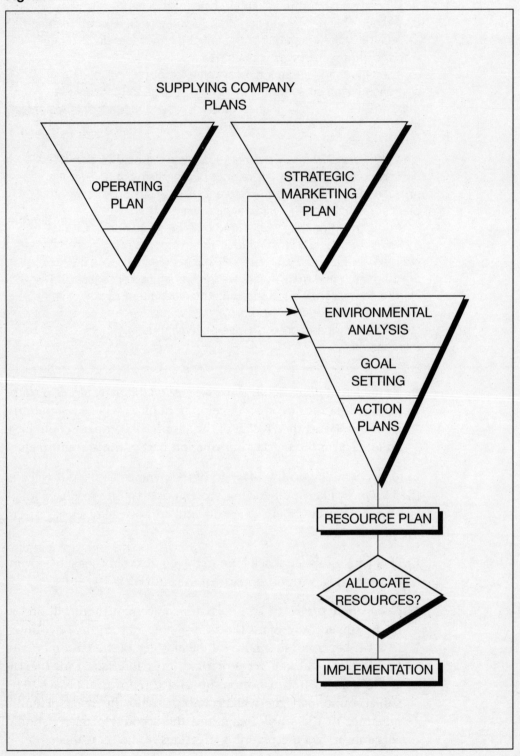

SUPPLYING COMPANY
PLANS

OPERATING
PLAN

STRATEGIC
MARKETING
PLAN

ENVIRONMENTAL
ANALYSIS

GOAL
SETTING

ACTION
PLANS

RESOURCE PLAN

ALLOCATE
RESOURCES?

IMPLEMENTATION

● *Divisional account plans.* If a division or subsidiary is big enough it may very well need its own sub-account plan. The team has to recognize this interface as well. The key is cross attendance at planning meetings, regularly rather than frequently.

I have a feeling that selling teams are making too little use of technology such as teleconferencing to help with this co-ordination of plans.

As we have already seen in Chapter 3, the last set of influencing plans belong to the customer. Figure 4.5 shows how the customer strategies and sub-account plans fit into the account planning process. I have also added in the sales campaigns. Any account plan will identify one or more key sales campaigns which, because of their complexity, will require a team or virtual team to get together to produce a sales plan. This completes the pyramid of plans.

> **If a division or subsidiary is big enough it may very well need its own sub-account plan.**

The schedule of planning events is important and I will give some examples of the theory and practice of this in the chapter on organization.

Draw your own pyramid of plans, identifying the key internal and external influencers of your account plan.

TRICKS OF THE TRADE

For the moment let us return to the mechanics and logistics of arranging a team planning event.

IS IT POSSIBLE TO MAKE A PRACTICAL PLAN AT THIS TIME?

Sometimes a planning session is mis-timed because an urgent issue or decision point needs to be resolved before further progress can be made. It is vital for the planning team to be open and honest in its assessment of the situation if the resulting plan is going to have what we are going to call "implementability". People are often surprised at how open a planning process has to be if it is to be successful.

Fig 4.5

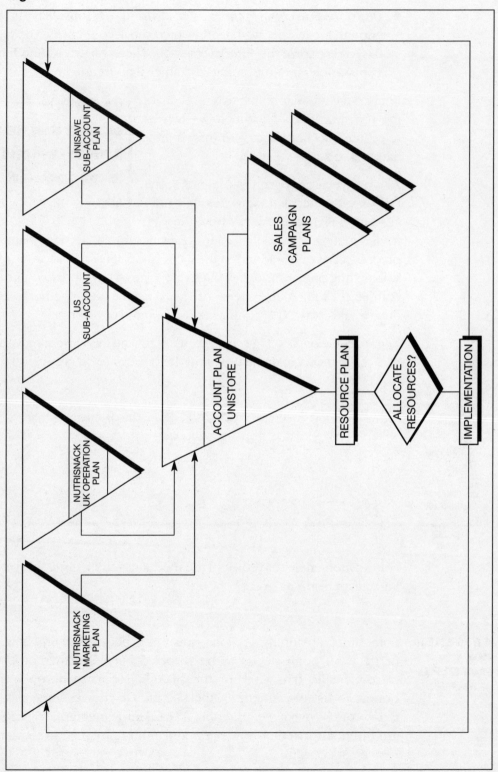

For the period of the planning session, rank and privilege must be broken down, and the team made to feel that everyone's contribution is important and will be considered when the plan is produced.

Account managers need to avoid the danger of producing a plan which will not succeed. A cause of this occurs when members of the team are inwardly stating "They can write that action down if they want, but I am not going to do it". Or "They can write that action down to me and I will not demur even though I know that I do not have the skills or knowledge to carry it out successfully".

In other words, an over riding consideration of any business planning process is "Is the plan going to be practical and is the team able and committed to executing it?"

EXAMPLE

No light in the electricity plan

A large utility was trying to break out of its cosy past where it had been a monopoly company wholly owned by the state, to a new situation where competition was about to become a reality. The managers of one of the biggest business units recognized two significant weaknesses.

They were over manned through some poor negotiation which had been circumscribed over many years by political considerations. They also did not have control over manning and pay issues, which historically had been handled at corporate level, with head office managers dealing with the leaders of the number of trade unions involved.

When the business unit managers were attempting to produce their business plan, this issue was ducked and the resultant plan was based on achievements on the employee relations side which were known to be impractical.

It would probably have been better to concentrate their planning energy on how to break this logjam. ○

This issue of *being in control* in sales planning terms is equally relevant. We must not produce a sales campaign which because of product, timescale or other issues is incapable of being won. Rather concentrate effort on removing the roadblock, or abandoning the campaign in the least damaging way.

Few people can plan effectively on their own. There are exceptions to this rule, but most people need the stimulus of others to get the creativity going, do some lateral thinking and come up with an imaginative plan.

WATCH OUT!

No team, but the room was the right size

I once worked with an account manager who worked for a major computer supplier and who turned up for a planning session I was facilitating on his own.

I introduced the process to him which he liked and bought into and he started work. The room he was in had a whiteboard all the way round it at a convenient height for writing.

During the next two days the account manager started at one side of the door and wrote down his plan on the whiteboard with little help from me.

By the end of the two days he had got round to the door again and declared his plan complete. He took photographs of the board, thanked me for my help and went off a happy man.

To this day I do not know how he knew so accurately how much whiteboard he would need. We must also remember that no-one else was committed to the action plans and the account manager had subsequently to get the buy-in of all the people whom he needed to carry out the action plans.

The result was not good. The account manager gave up trying to impose the plan on the rest of the organization and came back with the team for another go.

If there are permanent members of the selling team they will all have to be there. Support people or others who only make short-term contributions may sometimes be required.

The rule of thumb here is to decide whether the contribution of the person under consideration will be significant. Their presence also depends on the amount of authority the selling team has to make sure that that contribution is made.

If the actions are significant and the person needs to be persuaded to buy into his or her action plan, then you need to get them there early on in the process.

For key account plans and business plans, I find the concept of a "natural planning team" is helpful. Look at what needs to be achieved and suggest who you would naturally involve in such deliberations. The natural planning team is also useful to ensure that the level of detail you are going into is right for the people attending.

The concept of a "natural planning team" is helpful.

Make sure the right people are always discussing the right things

In a company which generates electricity, one of the natural planning teams is without any doubt the management team of each of the generating stations.

Each station has its own individual characteristics and it makes sense to produce the business plan by gathering together the senior managers and perhaps the next level as well.

During such a session the station management team will discuss the key issues concerning the generating plant. However, when it comes to producing the goals and activities required in the plant area, the whole station team may not be the "natural planning team". Do you really need the administration manager for such a technical activity?

In which case, the goal decided by the station team will be "To produce a plan for maintaining and improving the generating plant and equipment and report back to the station team within three months". This goal would be delegated to the appropriate natural planning team who will subsequently produce the plant plan using the same planning process if that is appropriate.

Failure to recognize this change in the natural planning team can cause frustration and a lack of efficiency in the planning session.

Avoid the "cast of thousands". An ideal planning number is probably between six and 10 persons, although where the natural planning team is greater I have worked successfully with as many as 30 people. Such numbers are the exception rather than the rule.

It is best to avoid asking observers or others who may be able to add information, but are not going to accept accountability for any part of the plan. We will discuss the level of knowledge you need for a key account plan and campaign plan in the chapters on those topics.

This is actually an impossible question to answer. Since no-one can know before the event takes place what the plan will contain, it is theoretically not possible to predict the time required.

Again from experience the most complex sales campaign plans rarely require more than two days to produce. They may take much less time. Particularly if you manage to get a good campaign planning process into the culture of the selling company, and people become comfortable and experienced. In this case a team may be able to formulate their plan in four to six hours.

A key account plan will take longer for the first pass and most people think that three days annually is the right amount of time to create the plan, and subsequently carry out a major review.

A business plan could take far longer, especially if the team is inexperienced in the process. I have a feeling that three days is a long enough stint at one go.

As we will discuss in later chapters, I prefer to run a three-day event. At the end the team agrees a set of actions for it to make further progress on the plan in smaller groups before coming together for one day to agree the first draft.

Do not forget that a plan is never "finished". The actions listed in the plan will be carried out with greater or lesser degrees of success and further iterations of the plan will go on for as long as the business exists or the account remains a key account.

There is no doubt that planning time saves activity time. A well structured and clear plan makes everyone involved work in a more focused and effective way. It allows the team to ensure that the whole is greater than the sum of the parts.

SETTING UP THE PLANNING ENVIRONMENT

Over years of helping literally hundreds of teams to produce plans, I have come to the conclusion that the place where the plan is created can have a significant impact on the quality of the plan.

Do not cramp people. I prefer a room which is suitable for at least twice as many people as are actually going to attend. Most people like lots of natural light, and I have found that a stuffy small room in the

> **Where the plan is created can have a significant impact on the quality.**

Never mind the plan, let's get on with doing things

A major telecoms company was faced with reviewing its sales organization and product portfolio to meet rapidly changing market conditions. Its culture at the time was a very action oriented one. Everyone at the top of the sales and marketing organization was very busy and working long hours.

They lacked planning disciplines, however, and therefore had a somewhat unfocused and unpredictable workload.

The senior manager involved, who was new to the company, asked me to facilitate a planning session for the reorganization. He also warned me that this lack of focus would lead to the team being distracted very easily to deal with some crisis. These were heralded, as often as not, by their mobile phones. His sales meetings, he said, tended to be attended haphazardly with people coming and going.

I organized the planning session in a hotel miles away from the team's normal working places, took out all the phones in the planning room and got the sales manager to instruct the team in no uncertain terms to be there and leave their mobile phones behind.

A mutinous band of highly talented people gathered at the appointed time and place. They were amazed that anyone should suggest that it might take three days for the plan to be completed. They felt that the time taken could much more wisely be spent actually getting on with meeting customers and producing individual documents for their own particular function.

The first breakthrough occurred when I said "OK, I will start you off on the process now and help you go through it as quickly as you can. The moment you feel comfortable that the plan is ready, we will stop. Even if you are happy with the plan in two hours time we will stop".

The second breakthrough occurred when they were still arguing about the current environment in the market after one full day. The process was more or less complete in the three days, but they had a series of actions to take which had to be done just to complete the plan.

They had more or less internalized the change and were prepared to give agreeing a team plan a chance. The problem then was to stop them reverting to their previous behaviour on returning to the field. ○

middle of a building with only neon lights can have an adverse effect on the planning team's demeanour. Simply, it becomes a rather depressing environment especially if the team is tackling an issue which is difficult to resolve.

If you are using a hotel room, check that all the lights work if you are going to need them at any time during the planning day. It is surprising how often as much as 20 per cent of the bulbs are blown and this has a significant impact on the brightness of the room.

Some people can only work if they are drinking coffee or tea, in which case you need a constant supply of the stuff in the room. I prefer to take a break every one-and-a-half or two hours, come out of the planning room and enjoy the change of environment. This becomes more necessary as fewer companies allow smoking in their meeting rooms. If you do have smokers they will appreciate an opportunity to go where smoking is permitted.

In any case, try to stop them getting to the phones or being distracted by secretaries or other people arriving during the breaks. I deliberately make the breaks unpredictable to avoid such disturbance.

I do not encourage people to take notes individually. I much prefer the notes of the planning meeting to be flip charts which slowly but surely record the conclusions of the team in full view of everyone. That way there can be no misunderstanding about what was agreed.

This brings me to the last point concerning the room. The team is going to hang the flip charts round the walls of the room – so make sure that the walls are suitable for such treatment – it can be expensive if the tape you use to stick the charts up removes bits of Louis XV wallpaper when they are torn down.

USING A FACILITATOR IN THE PLANNING PROCESS

If the easy answer to the question "When should we use a formal planning process?" is "Whenever you need to". The easy answer to "When should we use a facilitator?" is "Whenever he or she can add value".

It is hard to define a rule which states in what circumstances a facilitator would be appropriate. Account managers who understand how such sessions work are likely to get better at judging when it is appropriate to use the services of an outsider, versed in the intricacies of team planning.

Use a facilitator:

- **When a significant number of members of the team are unfamiliar with the process.**

- **When an outsider's view may remove blockages to planning.**

- When an outsider's view may help the team to raise its vision from the day-to-day problems of running the business.

- When an outsider's view may prevent the team ducking issues.

- When an outsider's view may bring experience from similar planning sessions.

Do not use a facilitator:

- To handle issues which are straightforward people management issues.

- If the team is not serious about building a plan for which they intend to become accountable.

A facilitator from outside may bring the following benefits:

- *Organization.* An experienced facilitator will help with the set-up of the session and the accurate setting of expectations.

- *Guidance.* Previous experience allows the facilitator to guide the team through the process and look for short cuts where possible

- *Discipline.* An outside facilitator is in a good position to insist on the essential planning disciplines designed to ensure the efficiency of the session.

- *Vision.* An outsider, lacking the knowledge and prejudices of the planning team, can help to keep up the vision of the team, discover new creative ideas and foster a "can-do" team attitude. Facilitators who are working with many different companies gain an unusual insight into what is fashionable or what are the current trends and pressures in business generally.

- *Team building.* An outsider can assist with team building as an arbiter and asker of hard questions.

- *Adaptability.* If the facilitators are active with a number of teams they will be able to adapt the process and content of the sessions as market and internal company issues change.

At the end of the session the team will decide how to keep the process alive and if and how it wishes to use the outside facilitation in the future.

The upside down triangle tries to show diagramatically the timing of a planning session. If it takes one unit of time to agree the goals, one hour, one day, one week or whatever, it will take three to do the environmental analysis and about half a time unit to do the action plans.

Sales teams tend to be very activity-oriented and may find this process slightly laborious the first time through. During the SWOT analysis they will see an awful lot of key issues which they know are going to lead to an awful lot of activity. They quite often feel a bit down at the end of the first day. Live with it.

They will eventually get to goal setting and activity planning and experience shows that the quality of the plan is directly related to the quality of the environmental analysis.

Remain flexible

To be frank, it doesn't much matter if an issue is recorded as a weakness or a threat. As long as the issue is recorded it will impact the plan, so do not be rigid. If you realize that the team is making a mistake, ask questions to enable them to see what is going wrong, but do not dwell on it.

Quite often poor sentences remain on the wall for a couple of days and then suddenly get corrected. We can always rectify mistakes later.

> **As long as the issue is recorded it will impact the plan.**

Remember, it is their plan and they will be responsible for implementing it. The only person who doesn't need to be in 100% agreement with the plan is the facilitator.

The more plans the facilitator is involved in, however, the more ideas he or she will cross-fertilize into new plans. This is a good thing as it improves the quality of plans and saves time.

Teams with problems

If they are struggling, it is almost certainly because the previous element of the planning process has not been comprehensively or well done.

If they are having problems activity planning, maybe the goal is too broad or not specific enough. If they are having problems setting goals, it is probably because the environmental analysis is incomplete or rushed. If they are struggling with the environmental analysis, it is almost certainly because they do not have enough hard or soft data, ie they don't know enough about the customer.

In such a case, curtail the planning session to a simple activity plan for finding out the necessary information.

Watch for low responders and very deliberately make them contribute. Watch for dominators and make them listen to the rest of the team. With the latter, it is sometimes necessary to have a word off line.

Vision

Make them keep the vision up. If the plan is becoming unrealistic, we will detect it at activity planning time and change it. Most plans err on the side of being highly achievable but not sufficiently stretching. The role of the facilitator is to balance that out.

FAST TRACK

○ *Decide on at least one complex campaign where you need to get the selling team together formally to produce a plan.*

○ *If you were going to produce a key account plan for one of your accounts, where would you start? Is it feasible to create a plan for the whole account, or should you start with the subsidiary or part of the account you understand best?*

5

planning winning sales campaigns - 1

creating, updating and implementing a plan for a complex sales situation

---

The long-term relationship with the customer is the account manager's overall aim, but the supplying company needs sales. Most sales in this environment are complex in that they involve many people in the buying and selling process. Both the buying team and the selling team could be spread nationally and internationally.

objectives and organization of a campaign plan

First, the objectives of planning for complex sales:

- **To agree the starting point from the prospect's point of view.**

- **To agree the starting situation of the selling organization.**

- **To agree the overall objective(s) of the campaign.**

- **To set milestones on the way to the objective in order to be able to monitor the implementation of the plan.**

- **To identify the resources required to implement the plan and win the business.**

- **To produce a detailed list of actions required to win the business.**

- **To identify skills deficiencies in the sales team.**

- **To get the team's and management's complete buy-in to the action plans and resource plan.**

The process I am about to describe is relevant for any sales campaign which can be said to be complex. As a rule of thumb, a complex sale is one where there are a number of people involved in the buying process and a team involved in selling.

Having decided that on the face of it the campaign is about business which we want and which we can win, we can start to organize the process.

GETTING THE TIMING RIGHT

It is of little value to call the team together before the customer has reached, either with you or without you, that part of the buying cycle which identifies the objective of some putative investment.

You can be too late as well. To pull the team together just as the customer is about to make a decision also leads to a less productive planning session. There is frankly little that can be done to influence the way the campaign is going, and the team will simply produce a situation report which will record the fact that they are likely to win or likely to lose.

The best test for the right time to get into the process is whether or not the selling team can produce a meaningful campaign goal. The team needs to be able to state what they are going to try to sell and what overall benefit the customer is going to gain.

Experience shows that the right time to do the original plan is when the customer is at least some way through the buying cycle but some significant time away from the decision on suppliers.

Common sense should tell us when we need to get the team together.

If we take a lengthy buying cycle then probably we should consider the time right when the customer is at least three months from a decision date but not more than nine months away.

These matters are complicated by customers frequently being unable to put down and stick to a decision date but common sense should tell us when we need to get the team together.

SETTING THE CAMPAIGN GOAL

Getting this first step right is a vital part of the planning process. It enables the team to focus its efforts on an agreed aim and allows the account manager to check with the customer that he or she is reading the situation correctly.

As with all objective setting which we will deal with in this book, a campaign goal must obey the following rules. To be an acceptable statement of the team's aim, a goal must be SMART:

- **S**tretching.
- **M**easurable.
- **A**chievable.
- **R**elated to the customer.
- **T**ime targeted.

Stretching

There is no point in wasting precious selling time on planning a sale which is going to occur even if the selling team went on a cycling tour of the Scottish Highlands. The job has to be difficult enough to merit the time required to set the plan.

Further, it is the role of the account manager to change the world. He or she needs to set goals which test the ability of the team to be persuasive, ie to change the mind of the customer to do something different or larger.

I have frequently found that a good campaign planning session will change or add to the goal as the team examines what the opportunities are. If this happens it is indeed right to change the goal. With all elements of the plan, you need to remain flexible to an ever changing environment and new ideas. The overall goal is no exception to this rule.

Universal Systems Integrators is going to run a major sales campaign to sell products and services to a major electricity company. The goal starts off stretching enough:

To sell £1,350,000 of hardware and £1,500,000 of systems consultancy, design and implementation.

Measurable

The normal measure of a campaign goal is a sum of money which the team is going to achieve in sales revenues or in profits.

In theory the team should be interested in both and set a target which predicts the order value and the resultant profit. In practice many companies, for good reasons, do not give the profit responsibility to the account manager and he or she may not be able to predict profitability.

There is much to be said on both sides of this debate, and we will return to it in the chapter on the organization and motivation of the account team. As stated above the objective is already measurable.

In most cases it is unlikely that the selling company can be very accurate with figures at this stage. The team needs, however, to make an estimate to ensure that the plan is worth doing and that they can get a rough grip of what products and services will be required to solve the customer problem.

Achievable

Having made certain that the goal is stretching, the team must also believe that it can be achieved. Normally a customer is planning capital investment all the time, and the selling team should be sufficiently close to the customer to recognize where there is a feasible chance of success.

The achievable test is particularly important where totally new technology is envisaged which the customer will recognize as carrying extra risk. I have often seen salespeople seeing an opportunity, proving a good business case and then losing because not enough people in the customer were willing to propose the risk to senior management.

The key to checking achievability is to ask the question of as many people as possible inside the customer and at as high a level as possible.

To sell £1,350,000 of hardware and £1,500,000 of systems consultancy, design and implementation.

In this case, the proposed solutions involve extension and amendment to systems which are already in place. There is little technology risk, but there are dangers involved in the enormous change which the organization and its people will have to accept and implement.

It will be stretching to help the customer face those risks, but on balance the objective looks achievable.

Related to the customer

Just as we must be able to see what is the benefit of the campaign for the selling company in terms of revenues and profits we must also get a flavour of what is in it for the customer.

In the action of checking the campaign goal with the customer, the wording of this can be useful in terms of getting the customer's agreement on the main benefit statement which the account manager will use in the sales campaign.

To sell £1,350,000 of hardware and £1,500,000 of systems consultancy, design and implementation of a call centre which in time will become the single interface to the company's customers. It will improve customer service and decrease the number of calls customers have to make to achieve a satisfactory result. At the same time the electricity company will reduce the costs and staffing levels of its current telephone response centres.

Time targeted

The date of the completion of the goal completes the rules of setting appropriate objectives.

Once again the concentration must be on the customer's view.

It is uncanny how many sales campaigns are targeted to end by the date of the completion of the selling company's financial year. Once again the concentration must be on the customer's view. Is the timescale suitable for him as well for the selling company?

We can assume that the team puts a sensible timescale on the objective.

Some account managers are uncomfortable with the prospect of showing the customer the basis for a sales campaign. They worry that the customer will baulk at a price given too early, or a timescale with which he cannot at this stage agree.

I do not understand the logic of this. In solution selling we are always trying to understand why the customer will not buy as well as why he will. The earlier we know about any objection in the mind of the customer the better we can make our plan to deal with it.

A simple trial close can give good return and add to the plan significantly.

Seller: "We are aiming to supply the solution for completion of the installation by the end of July."

Buyer: "No way. There will be a bottleneck on the engineering effort required which makes that date far too optimistic."

Seller: "If we could show you an implementation plan which identifies those engineering resources and gets implementation complete by July, would you consider it?"

The vigour with which the customer sustains this objection will tell the seller how feasible is the earlier date. In any case the discussion of the campaign goal has started the process well by identifying the concerns of the customer which, if not dealt with, will become objections to the sale.

the campaign planning process

If we take the general planning model from Chapter 4 it is relatively simple to express the three elements of a campaign plan.

In the case of a campaign, the environmental analysis concerns the customer's buying cycle, the customer's reasons for buying and our qualification of the project. Qualifying the prospect deals with whether we can win the business and whether the profit available is worth the effort we will have to put in. Expressed as a ▼ it looks like the following:

Fig 5.1

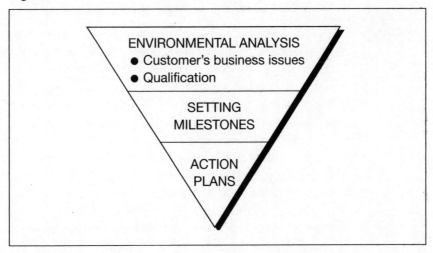

When it comes to setting milestones for our progress in the sale, they are best divided into two types: the customer's business issues and our people issues.

In this way we are pursuing both the logic of the sale, ie what is in it for the customer, but also the psychological and people issues which are the focus of the skill of selling.

Both areas are essential. If we do not assist the customer to prove his business case, someone else may and if that someone else is a competitor then he will be gaining competitive advantage.

Besides, if there is no real financial and strategic reason for the customer to buy, someone in the organization is going to call a halt. This person is frequently quite high in the company and the damage done is more than wasted selling effort, it is also the loss of reputation with an influential person. Their first impression of the selling company is that it pursues sales for its own exclusive benefit rather than checking that there is something in it for the customer as well.

If proof were needed that suppliers as well as customers must pay attention to the business case, this story illustrates it. Not only has the IT manager damaged his image, so have the suppliers. The suppliers have also wasted a lot of effort on a project which may never now get off the ground.

Customers do not buy technology, they buy solutions

The technical team of a large company was looking at the technologies on offer to change radically its plant maintenance routines. It became obvious that with a better system for recording the history of plant in terms of its life cycle would give benefits in terms of the quality and reliability of its deliveries to its customers. This was without any doubt strategic to the organization which was trying to become more competitive in exactly that area of the business.

A technical committee invited IT companies and consultants to come in and look at the problem. No less than seven companies decided to bid for the business.

Suppliers and customer became entangled in the intricacies of a most interesting problem, and various imaginative solutions were proffered. The technical committee rejected some of these and came up with a short list of possibilities.

The remaining companies still tendering went into top gear. More detailed investigation followed until everyone was able to produce a presentation of their method of taking the company from its outdated method of organizing its plant maintenance to the golden automated future.

The business case rested very heavily on the strategic requirement to produce better customer satisfaction. The cashflow did not take into account how this would be reflected in the performance of the business. No-one had, hand on heart, given an estimate of the extra sales which would follow the improvement. In fact, the cashflow showed continued negative return for all 10 years of the expected life of the project.

The IT manager in charge needed a Board decision to spend a modest amount of money on some consultancy work which would take the project to its next stage. The chairman of the Board went straight to the cashflow, found that it was negative £7,000,000 after 10 years and asked why on earth they should do the project.

The IT manager was then completely on the back foot. He had an uphill struggle to convince a sceptical Board that new estimates of growth of business made the project worthwhile. The Board will accept that type of estimate with a pinch of salt. How will it know if the benefit to the customer comes through as a benefit to the company? Besides, if the project has such good strategic return why was it not identified earlier?

Fig 5.2

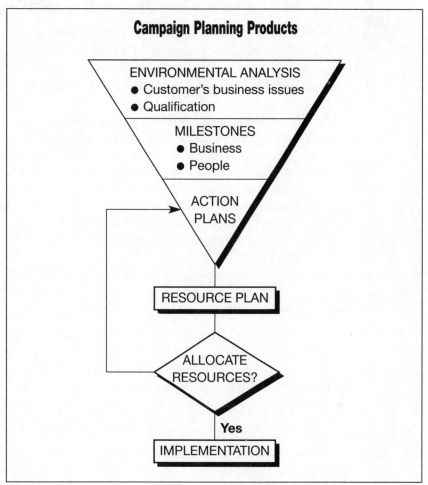

Another problem which the inevitable delay of a poor business case causes the supplier, is an internal one. The account

The suppliers have also wasted a lot of effort.

manager probably twisted arms and struggled to ensure the availability of the resources to do the next step.

The embarrassment of delay will also turn into a loss of credibility the next time the acount manager wants resource.

A project is frequently delayed because of the lack of a good business case for the customer. But the people issues are equally important.

The attitude of the decision-makers counts as well as the logic of the proposal

The fact of the matter in this plant maintenance case is that the Board had two identifiable sets of individuals, the "hard-liners" and the "deal sensitively with the staff and make progress step by step people persons".

The hard-liners were bound to reject any project which did not show advantages in profitability as well as in customer services. The other members were much more amenable to a vaguer approach which did not force staff into predictions of financial benefits which were extremely difficult to make or at least to get right.

The chief executive was the decision-maker. If he had answered the chairman's question by backing up the IT manager's claim of strategic benefit, the project would probably have gone ahead. In this case he was sympathetic to the hard-liners and wanted the concrete numbers to be tabled and someone made responsible for their achievement.

It is plain that the suppliers were unaware of this grouping on the Board or what action the chief executive was likely to take. The people side as well as the business side of campaign planning was missing and they all paid the penalty.

Once the selling team can see what it needs to achieve to win the business it can start the activity plans (see page 73).

The key to getting the activity plans practical is accountability. Each action must have an owner who has accepted the job and the timescale for it.

If they are not there, they are not committed

A supplier of telecommunication equipment was trying to break into a new market by selling a combination of hardware and software to give additional functionality to its customer. The sales team met and set the milestones for the complex sale. Unfortunately some key people were not there.

Since the service being bid was new, quite a lot of resource had to achieve a number of reasonably difficult changes to the normal product. This needed the agreement of the marketing people who had to believe that this first sale would be followed by others.

The sales team assumed that the pressure of the customer requirement would be irresistable and included in the plan a series of activities for the marketing department.

▶

Add to this the effort required from the developers of the products and it is easy to see why the publication of the plan was the starting point of a huge row.

Only people involved in the creation of the plan can be assigned actions. If other resources are required to make a contribution, then a member of the planning team is given the action to liaise with the managers of those resources and get their agreement to the action and the timescale.

resource planning and the management review process

Any planning process ends up with a number of goals or milestones and a series of actions which the team is committed to take to achieve these aims. Resource planning should be a simple resort of the activities by resource.

The team knows what results it is striving for and has established what it needs to do. It is now in a position to inform management of the plan. It takes its resource plan to the managers responsible for the required resources of people, machinery and money. A decision is made.

This is a crucial time in the life of the plan. When the selling team, makes its presentation both sides, management and the team, must be clear whether the review is to look at the quality of the plan or whether it is to commit resources to the implementation.

Management will have lots of submissions to look at. If it is the stage of the financial year where it is reviewing plans all round the organization before making decisions on resources, it must make this absolutely clear to the teams.

In too many cases teams have a feeling that management has agreed the resources where in fact the management were still examining all the possibilities. We will examine this further in the chapter on organization.

Let us assume that both management and the team are certain that a review meeting is going to make decisions on resources. Lots can still go wrong, particularly in an organization which is in the throes of putting formal planning into its selling teams.

The best way to approach the meeting is in terms of a contract. The selling team proposes the result which it believes it can achieve, as we have said normally measured by sales revenues and/or profit. It also produces the resource plan which it believes is required if the goal is to be achieved.

> **The best way to approach the meeting is in terms of a contract.**

It is management's prerogative to question and suggest change to the action plans and therefore resource plans. It is in a position to suggest work which has been done elsewhere and which could offer the selling team some shortcuts.

Very significantly it is in a position to know whether or not the resources requested have the necessary knowledge, skills and experience to carry out the actions assigned to them. This too can change or, in extreme cases, invalidate the plan.

In the end the agreement is made and the contract accepted. "We will give this result if you will give us these resources." There is an important point still to be remembered by both sides. All contracts, particularly stretching contracts, are taken in good faith with "best intentions" on both sides.

Sometimes one or other of the parties will fail. Just as the selling team can give no guarantees of success in a competitive world, so management will sometimes fail in its endeavours to provide the promised resource. A missed deadline on a product improvement, for example, is going to occur. The key is for both sides to recognize and acknowledge the risks.

The whole thing can go hopelessly wrong if the company culture becomes one of less than openness by either or both parties.

If the selling team gets the impression that any proposal it makes is going to be accepted as good by management, but that it will then require the team to achieve it with much less resource than is in the plan, then the selling team will add a little to the resource plan, knowing that it will be cut.

If the management team feels that any proposal which the selling team makes will be less than can be achieved and take more resources than actually required, then a vicious circle starts.

Worse still, opportunities will be lost where the selling team makes an assumption that the resources will not be available to exploit them.

In a mature planning organization the results are stretching but achievable, the resources sensible and expected to work profession-ally. In such a case this initial review will produce an agreed contract which with best efforts will succeed.

Further reviews will occur as time passes, the team makes progress and things change. We will look at this continuous reviewing process after going through in detail each step in the creation of the plan.

FAST TRACK

○ *Choose one of the sales campaigns which you intend to produce a plan for, and establish the "SMART" goal for the campaign.*

○ *Decide when and with whom in the customer you are going to check the goal.*

○ *Decide on a timetable for going through the creative planning process and ending with a management review.*

6

planning winning sales campaigns - 2

analyzing the environment to understand the customer's starting point and business issues

_____

The major difference between a product salesperson and a solution selling account manager is the depth of understanding that the account manager brings to the customer's real needs.

In this chapter we will look at the first part of the planning process: the customer environmental analysis. For most steps I will give examples from many different situations which I have seen over the years.

In the appendix there are copies of the checklists involved and examples taken from completed campaign plans. If your teams use computers, it makes sense to think about presenting the checklists and other documents in computer form.

step by step through the campaign planning process

By now the account manager has in mind a campaign goal and has agreed with an appropriate senior manager in the customer that it obeys the rule of being a "SMART" objective. The account manager needs now to assemble the team to validate the goal and produce the campaign plan.

By now the account manager has in mind a campaign goal.

This chapter will cover the process with the following steps:

- **How long the team should allow.**

- **Prior to the event.**

- **Assessing the customer's business issues.**

In Chapter 7, I will cover the next steps of qualification and evaluation.

As you look at these checklists and, I hope, try to envisage them in use in one of your accounts, remember that a planning session is never based on a complete set of facts. In common with all business decisions there is always an element of the unknown.

As you discover holes in your knowledge base, note them down in the plan. Then when you come to action planning you can put one of the team members in charge of collecting the facts which are missing.

You are going to have to work with a less than perfect knowledge database, but this checklist should help you to recognize the gaps, plan to fill them or plan your way round them. After all "forewarned is forearmed".

HOW LONG THE TEAM SHOULD ALLOW

As pointed out earlier this is a difficult question to answer. If the team is new to the process and the campaign goal is big enough to merit it, you should allow two days. This is sufficient time to do a thorough job on the environmental analysis, decide as a team the milestones involved in achieving the goal and agree an action plan. It is also enough time to prepare and carry out a management review, either to inform management of the plan or to obtain agreement to the resource plan.

Although in theory a team should continue with the process for as long as it takes for them to be satisfied with the quality of the work, in practice most teams need a time target. The prior agreement of a manager to attend a briefing at say 3.45pm on the second day gives a useful focus to the event. The team is aware that it needs to have something sensible to say before that time.

The timescale for an audit of an existing plan is shorter, say a day or even a more regular half day. The chapter on organization and review will look deeper at the audit function while this chapter is mainly concerned with the creation of a new plan.

PRIOR TO THE EVENT

Here is a checklist of what needs to be done before the campaign planning is started in earnest.

Get the agreement of the team members and their management that they are committed to attend

Try to do this well in advance and confirm the arrangement in writing. Planning tends to demonstrate its benefits some time after it has been done. You always run the risk therefore that a crisis which can be solved in the short term gets a higher priority on the actual day of the planning event.

The planning team should include anyone who will be involved in the implementation of the plan and take accountability for some of the actions.

Agree a time for an appropriate manager to come to hear the plan review

The most appropriate manager is the one who has the authority to agree all the resources. This person may not be available because of the number of plans he or she would have to review, and compromise may be necessary. It is certainly useful for the manager to have some control over some of the required resources.

In most cases it is desirable that the manager is more senior to everyone in the team including the account manager

Send out a briefing document to all team members

Make sure that everyone is aware of the objectives of the planning event and of the putative campaign goal which the account manager is going to propose. Set their expectations for what the event will have as its output.

Emphasize that it is not only a think-tank but also a decision-making forum where they are going to be asked to commit themselves to actions and accountability for their completion.

Include in the briefing the minimum of information necessary for the team to be aware of the customer opportunity and have a passing knowledge of your company's relevant products and services. The event itself is not the appropriate time to go into great detail, particularly on technical issues, so keep it short and simple.

Articles about the opportunity and an overview of the customer for those who are unfamiliar with it is all that is needed.

Agree the customer input

Unlike account plans, campaign plans are normally created without reference to the customers. After all, you are going to get into detailed areas of politics and people, yours and theirs.

It is a shame however to miss the opportunity to impress customers with the professionalism of the process you are going to use. They will probably be interested **Invite the customer to make a contribution.** also in the fact that you and your company are taking the campaign seriously.

In this regard you may get further confirmation of how seriously the customer is approaching the matter. Few customer managers wilfully allow a supplier to go to the sort of trouble and expense of running a planning session unless there is some intention on their part to do something about the problem or opportunity.

It is often, therefore, a good idea to invite the customer to make a contribution to the plan, perhaps as an after dinner speaker on the topic or during the event itself. If you are inviting the customer, make sure you brief them as well.

Choose a good location

There is not much to add to what is in Chapter 4 on planning rooms. Make sure you have plenty of flip chart paper and many different coloured pens.

If it is possible, bring the technology with you to allow a member of the team or someone brought in specially for the task to produce the paper document at the end of the first day. This document is the hard copy of what the team has produced in flip chart form. It is very straightforward to put the template (which is produced in full in the appendix) on to a computer

Choose and brief a facilitator

Chapter 4 suggested the advantages of using an outside facilitator in planning. In this context outside means someone from outside the team. Building a small group of people who become experienced in facilitating these sessions will pay great dividends as the facilitators pass experience and ideas from one part of the organization to another.

In a number of organizations such people are often recruited from the training department. This makes good sense as they will already have the skills in controlling groups, asking questions and dealing with questions and difficulties.

There is as usual a potential down-side with using the training department. An experienced team of salespeople may challenge the credibility of someone who has never sold, or even of someone who has not been in selling for a while.

Match those requirements, however, and trainers can become very useful resources with well-developed facilitating skills which will add considerabe value to any planning event.

You should brief the facilitator in the same way as the rest of the team. In addition you will need to brief him or her on the people in the team. Be open about the strengths and weaknesses of the team members. If you suspect that the facilitator may hit problems with one or two people, it is much better to warn him or her in advance.

The first responsibility is to look at the customer requirement and ask searching questions about why the customer will buy from a business point of view. The checklist looks like this:

- What is the customer's business objective for this campaign?

- What critical success factors declared by the customer does this campaign address?

- What benefits, both tangible and intangible, will the customer derive from a successful implementation?

- What are the rough costs of all the expenditure involved?

- How does the *prima facie* return on investment look?

- What key ratios will be the basis of how the customer measures the success of the project?

- Where in terms of geography and company divisions will the benefits occur?

- What are the risks which the customer will take if it goes ahead with this project?

- How does the size of this project compare with others the customer has undertaken?

What is the customer's business objective for this campaign?

In order to sell into the heart of a company and its direction, you need to understand how the project you are proposing fits into the company's strategy and direction. Use this question to try to compose a single sentence which connects the project with a major company strategy or vision.

Getting the customer's business objective for the project right is important. It sets the theme of how we are going to interest and sell to every level of management in the organization. It is also a very shortcut method of briefing anyone from the selling company on the overall reason why the customer is going to buy.

If you have decided to involve the customer in your planning event, you may be able to agree this statement there and then.

Getting the customer's business objective for the project right is important.

EXAMPLE

Connect your selling proposition to the heart of the customer's business

Taking the example of Burton's strategy statements from Chapter 2:

○ Building a powerful brand around a total fashion approach,

○ we increased profits through the tighter management of stock and a substantial reduction in markdowns.

If we were selling something into this environment we would propose an objective such as:

To stock a new line of garment which takes the total fashion approach a stage further, and increases profits by agreeing a just-in-time delivery from the supplier. ○

One further reason for working hard on this question is that as you develop the solution which you are going to sell, it is a prime checking point in maintaining the customer focus of your plan. As you make changes to what you are going to propose, check back with this statement to ensure that you have not subtly changed the likely impact on the customer.

What critical success factors declared by the customer does this campaign address?

Now broaden your search for how well the project fits the customer strategy. You need to understand from published material or from questioning the customer what issues are believed to be critical to the customer achieving his or her business objectives.

These are frequently identified in the company's annual report. Starting from there you need to check again at the highest level possible whether the CSFs (critical success factors) are still current. Such a conversation will also give you other ideas for fitting the project to the customer strategy.

Here are some examples of CSFs which could be built into various different proposals for capital investment or other type of purchase.

From the report and accounts of a large food manufacturer:

"The driving force which made restructuring so necessary was change, in market dynamics as well as technology."

"Following a major reassessment of corporate strategy, we have increased focus on those product categories and regions which we believe offer the greatest potential for profitable growth."

Both of these statements give a selling team an opportunity to connect its sales campaign to the heart of the customer's business.
  Incidentally, in account management terms the second statement leads to a couple of interesting questions. Which products and regions does the company see as potential for profitable growth? If it is not our product area or regional specialization, our chances for success are lowered, although our chances of being in a low-chance selling campaign remain as high as ever. ○

What benefits, both tangible and intangible, will the customer derive from a successful implementation?

This is a straightforward list of all the potential benefit areas. It distinguishes tangible benefits from intangible. The difference is that tangible benefits can be reduced to a sum of money whereas intangible benefits can be seen as useful, but not quantifiable. The point was made in the previous chapter that tangible benefits are much more persuasive to a board of directors than intangible.

It is not possible to produce a comprehensive list of tangible and intangible benefits but here are some thought provokers:

Tangible benefits

- Reduction of costs
  - Staff savings
  - Accommodation savings
  - Transport costs
  - Power costs
  - Other consumables
  - Equipment
  - Current systems
  - Administration
  - Insurance.

Less tangible benefits
(These are less easy to make into a believable estimate)

- Increased sales.

- Reduced stocks.

- Avoid additional costs
  - Administration
  - Systems
  - Promotional costs
  - Marketing.

Intangible benefits

- Staff morale.

- Job satisfaction.

- Customer satisfaction.

- Product reliability.

FAST TRACK

○ *Make a list of the benefit areas which your products and services normally provide as a checklist for campaign planning.*

What are the rough costs of all the expenditure involved?

This list needs to be comprehensive. Make sure that there are no hidden extras. It is not possible to produce a general list for costs as they obviously vary enormously dependent on the type of sales campaign.

Make sure that there are no hidden extras.

FAST TRACK

○ *Tailor your list to give a comprehensive checklist of the costs involved in buying your products and services.*

Here is a representative list for a technology project.

One-off costs	Ongoing expenditure
Equipment purchase	Staff
Room preparation	Equipment rental
Furniture	Accommodation
Installation	Maintenance
Training and familiarization	Training
	Consumables
	Energy
	Communications

How does the prima facie return on investment look?

Even at this stage you and the customer can make a first draft of the cost benefit analysis. The main holes in the case are likely to be in estimating the tangible benefits.

In the action plan which follows you will put down activities such as meetings with line managers to gain their agreement to the quantification of the business case.

What key ratios will be the basis of how the customer measures the success of the project?

Directors and managers at all levels of a business have in their minds a number of key ratios. For example, first line sales managers will be aware at most times what their sales revenues are to date compared to where they should be at this time of the company year.

Solution selling demands that we understand what financial ratios each of the key people holds important. From that knowledge we can tailor the presentation of benefits to illustrate the impact on those ratios which are personally important.

We will not always be successful, as no project can be expected to hit the hot buttons of every executive involved, but it is a good challenge to try to be as comprehensive as possible.

Managers take very different views of their key ratios, and once again it is not possible to give a comprehensive list. Do not forget also, that they will change with time and the environment. What was a key ratio when there was little price pressure will be irrelevant when gross margins are being squeezed by competition.

EXAMPLE

Key performance ratios

A generating station manager in an electricity company looks at cost per unit of electricity and plant availability. These are compared regularly with targets set at the beginning of the company year.

A production manager looks at the ratio of stock held to sales revenues.

A senior manager of a consultancy organization looks at the ratio of revenue earning days of each consultant compared with non-productive administration and selling days.

Food store managers look at a series of detailed information about shelf space and sales.

A department store manager is interested in the ratio of cross-selling to original purchases. ○

FAST TRACK

○ *Look at the ratios your products and services are likely to impact for each of the functions liable to be involved in the buying process. Use these as a checklist for this part of the campaign planning process.*

Where in terms of geography and company divisions will the benefits occur?

If the product you are selling is going to have a wide impact, it is necessary to make a good list of where the benefits must be sold. At some point you need a groundswell of opinion moving towards a recommendation for your product, and the wider and louder this ground swell is, the better the chances of success.

Getting the support of global line management

An advertising agency is bidding for a worldwide account. The buying company's strategy is "globalization". This means that the Board would like to use an advertising campaign which can be used with only language changes.

In this context the account manager for the agency will want to use his or her local teams in all parts of the world where the advert is to be used, to check over the design process.

This demonstrates two things about the agency's bid:

○ It can, because it is globally spread itself, carry out this task.

○ It can use relationships at local level to act as champions of its bid.

Now put yourself in the position of another agency bidding for the same business. It does not have a worldwide presence but relies on co-operation with local agencies in those countries where the buying company wishes to advertise.

If it fails to recognize where it needs support, apart from at the centre, it runs competitive risk. The ground swell from abroad will make a centralized (or *imposed* as the countries abroad will feel) decision in its favour impossible.

Take the benefits message to all concerned

By its very nature a telecommunications company is selling to its key accounts a global solution. Once again the places where the benefits of a proposal for a worldwide network will be felt needs examination to ensure that the necessary contacts are made.

There is frequently a feeling in subsidiary companies and divisions which operate in a different country from head office that head office does not understand the local situation, or that interference from head office is somehow reducing their responsibility for their own destinies.

However, a centrally devised infrastructure service, like the telecommunications network makes more sense if it comes as a result of a consistent strategy.

The job of the account manager in this environment is to recognize the politics and set a plan which ensures that the benefits of the proposal are accepted widely.

What are the risks which the customer will take if it goes ahead with this project?

This is not the detailed risk analysis which a company looks at in calculating return on investment, but more a strategic look at the risks involved. Use the strategy state-

A strategic look at the risks involved.

ments from above such as the company's objective for the project or the company's CSFs as a guide to this part of the exercise.

Is this project, while consistent in theory with the buying company's strategy and CSFs, putting any of these areas at risk?

EXAMPLE

Look for spin-off disadvantages

Take the case of the electricity company thinking about a Call Centre system. Is there any risk that the overall efficiencies achieved will damage the company's interface with, for example, remotely based customers?

If the Call Centre does everything management wants in the cities and towns of their market, but lets down an elderly community in a rural location all the customer satisfaction benefits will be lost.

This is not to mention the outrage of the political opposition who will seize on this mistake as a reason to question the whole Call Centre strategy.

These risks need to be assessed up front so that the customer is taking well-informed decisions and the selling company understands the emphasis to be placed in the solution which it eventually decides to sell. ○

How does the size of this project compare with others the customer has undertaken?

The reason for this question is that it is part of the start of the selling company's qualification process. With the best will and business case in the world, companies remain fearful of the unknown or the new.

There is a big difference between examining the technical and financial case for putting in a huge new way of doing things, and taking the decision to do it. It is always easier to sell the second implementation than the first. Equally it is always more likely that a company will go ahead with a project if it has done something of similar size before.

If this is a bigger or more geographically spread venture than the customer has attempted before, the selling team needs to take that into account in planning the campaign. Very deliberate actions will be put in place to try to build up the confidence of the customer that the project implementation will be successful.

Indeed it may be very desirable to identify this risk in more detail. It is not unusual to suggest that the customer buys some consultancy services to look at contingent risks brought on by a project.

FAST TRACK

○ *Take a campaign which you are running at the moment and try to answer the questions in this checklist.*

○ *Make a list of the questions you need to get answered to improve this.*

○ *Try a "post-hoc business case". Look at a sale which you have made in the past and try to answer the checklist questions based on that sale. This will demonstrate how close you were to the customer's strategic reasons for buying.*

7

planning winning sales campaigns - 3

analyzing the selling team's opening position and starting the continuous process of qualification

___

There is a Chinese proverb which states *"Before you decide where you want to go and how you are going to get there, make sure you know exactly where you are now"*. In account management you have to add *"and make sure everyone involved agrees"*.

Qualifying the prospect

Some would regard this part of the planning process as the most important. The qualification process never stops. Professional account managers are constantly assessing the changing position in the campaign. They are listening for signs, sometimes obvious sometimes subtle, which tell them how they stand against the competition.

The qualification process never stops.

What follows is the description of a checklist which probes into the areas where salespeople need to ask hard questions and acknowledge the answers, even those which say that all is not going well.

We will look at the process under the following headline questions:

- **Customer need.**
- **Finance.**
- **Key people.**
- **Timescale.**
- **Solution.**
- **Basis of decision.**
- **Implementability.**
- **Competitive position.**

Taking each of these one by one we will look at the subsidiary questions in each heading and use examples from a number of situations. There is a completed qualification checklist at the end of the chapter and a set of the checklist forms. Once again they are very suitable to be used as a computer-held template for future sales campaigns.

CUSTOMER NEED
In this section the team examines what progress has been made on the completion of a business case for the customer on which he could make a decision to buy. The subsidiary questions are:

Is it a real need?

The professional account manager is well aware that all managers and technicians are interested in new things. The purchasing department of a large retailer will have people who are constantly monitoring the market and the suppliers to it for new products.

Computer and telecommunications people at all levels are notorious for looking into new technologies, studying them until they understand them and then dropping their interest as something which is two keystrokes better comes along.

Selling teams are on their guard for timewasters and this question is a good starting point for establishing whether or not the prospect is seriously going to contemplate what you are proposing.

The best test is: "If you, the selling team, were running your customer's business, would you buy this product and go into this new environment?" If the answer to this is "Yes" then you have the start of a qualified prospect. If the customer at high level also expresses a real need for the solution then you have the beginnings of a runner.

A new technology is particularly difficult to get past this simple test. The fact is that if a company to date has found no need for a smart card which can also be used as a dialling card, then you are going to have to persuade a lot of executives to take the initial risk.

The selling team will have to prove that competitive disadvantage will occur for companies which do not get into the technology early. A stronger selling position would be to prove that a company will have competitive edge from leading the field.

Is the requirement strategic to the customer?

The work which the team has done in assessing the customer's business situation will tell it the strength of its situation in this regard. If, as suggested in the previous chapter, the team has already identified and sold the link between the project and the customer's strategy then the team will score well here.

If there are still a series of question marks or if there are any mismatches, then the team will recognize that a lot of work needs to be done before it can give itself a clean bill of health.

Swallowing the pill of a difficult qualifying decision

An advertising agency put a lot of effort into a bid for the business of the Singapore subsidiary of a global pharmaceuticals and chemicals company.

The team members had failed to understand that pharmaceuticals were no longer a strategic business to the corporation. They could have known this had they studied the published information or spoken to some senior managers at head office.

What they could not know was that the corporation was actively seeking a buyer for the pharmaceutical subsidiary.

In any case this was a very difficult campaign to qualify as the team would have had to understand the strategic aims of the account and then acted on it by dropping the campaign or slimming down their effort to a holding position. Probably under pressure from the Singapore company itself the decision to withdraw becomes even harder.

They continued to put the effort in, took the client to meet satisfied customers, made a proposal and laid on a professional and expensive presentation.

The bombshell dropped with the announcement that the corporation was involved in friendly talks with a possible buyer and all activities except the day-to-day continuation of trading were halted. ○

Is the campaign worth the necessary effort from the selling company?

This is the crunch. From the team's understanding of the customer's position and attitude to going forward with the project, it has to make a go or no-go decision. Not only that, but it has to revisit that decision on a regular basis as the customer's stance develops and changes.

The customer need is not the only issue involved in the decision on whether to put in sales effort or not. All the subsequent points related to the selling company and its situation will be taken into account as well.

But identifying a real need which is strategic for the customer to act on is the strongest basis for a campaign, and the absence of that is the weakest.

FINANCE

Is the money available in a budget?

Depending on the level of the account you are dealing with, you need to find out how budgets are set and whether some money is or could be allocated to the project you are selling.

Frequently, large companies have capital investment budgets separate from the day-to-day running budgets or revenue budgets. If it is possible, it is very desirable for an account manager to know how these budgets are set and to what level they are delegated.

The delegation issue is important. Some Boards will delegate portions of the capital investment budget to the next level of management, but insist that each major item of expenditure returns to them with a report and a recommendation on which they will then make a decision.

Other Boards will actually delegate the decision to the next level, or even lower. The trend as I write is towards more centralized control of capital expenditure budgets.

Having established where the budgets are, the selling team then has to answer the question: "Has money been allocated to this project?" or failing that: "Is there a reasonable chance that the money can be found?"

WATCH OUT!

Held back by a referral to another level

A salesperson was selling the Dialcard to the product development manager of a firm of stockbrokers. He carefully established that the manager concerned did have the authority to sign for a pilot scheme of £20,000. The budget was his and he had sufficient in his research and development fund to allocate the money to this project.

Unfortunately, he did not have the budget to fund the full project which, when the card went out to all customers, was going to cost some £100,000. His boss took the view that a decision on the pilot could only be taken if the people responsible for the larger amount were consulted and their agreement sought.

The result was much delay while the selling team demonstrated and sold the product to the sales and marketing department.

This was very difficult for the selling team to discover in the qualification process, but is a good example of how careful and wide you have to be in your questioning in this area.

Do all the people concerned have a rough cost expectation?

In the section on assessing the customer's business situation, we discussed the importance of letting everyone know what the cost of the project is likely to be. This sub question records whether or not the selling team has grasped the nettle or ducked the issue.

Once again level plays its part. It is not enough to find one manager who sees no problem in the money being found. Many salespeople have been blind sided by a senior manager stepping in at the last moment or at any time in the campaign with the dreaded question "How much?" said in a tone of disbelief.

Has the necessary return on investment process be completed?

In the qualification process this question is a summary of the customer's attitude to return on investment. Unusually it is a yes or no answer.

Any account which requires the attention of an account manager from a supplying organization will almost certainly have a business process for examining return on investment. With or without an account manager's knowledge, the buying company will put new projects through this process.

There are rarely exceptions. The process is, of course, sometimes unnecessary if the sum of money required is trivial. The team needs to identify the key person on the buying side who is responsible for this and ask the direct question "Has the project been evaluated, and did it pass?"

There is much debate among people involved in solution selling about this. Some people insist that it is too much like prying into the confidential business processes of the customer.

I am in agreement with the school that says that it is safer to be involved in this evaluation process than to take a risk. The risk is that activity is taking place inside the customer which could invalidate the sales campaign or some of the activities in the campaign plan.

As usual the customer holds the key. If you plan how to approach the customer with return on investment in mind, be prepared with the arguments as to why you need to be involved in the internal process.

The fact is that the account manager may very well be able to add value because of his or her knowledge of other companies who have gone down the same route. As we have seen, a professional account manager may be able to suggest costs which

Assist the buying team to assess or quantify the benefits of the proposition.

the buying team has not identified, or more important, assist the buying team to assess or quantify the benefits of the proposition.

Once the account manager has made an attempt to argue his or her way into involvement in the process, the customer will deliver judgement, and that seems to me the safest course.

When the arguments are not strong enough or there is a company policy which prohibits outsiders taking part in the financial exercise, the account manager will get a brush off, probably polite but decisive.

EXAMPLE

Even a "no" gives useful information

Here is the text of a letter from the finance director of an American multinational replying to a request from a supplier to be brought into the picture as to how the company performs return on investment.

Dear Ken

In reply to your letter of 6th May I would say that this company does not make public their processes for making financial decisions.

It may be helpful to point out that in our last quarter we announced return on equity of 25%. We also announced further progress in our endeavours to improve return on assets.

In these competitive days we examine carefully the NPV of any potential new spend.

I hope that this is of some use to you.

Yours sincerely

Finance Director

Ken has not done enough to get inside these confidential processes, but he has done his campaign no harm, and in the process got some authoritative opinions on what financial ratios are important to the company. If nothing else he has strengthened that part of the planning process which assesses the reasons the customer will buy. ○

Under the topic basis of decision, we will look at finding out the return on investment processes. This question is quite concrete: "Has the necessary return on investment process been completed?"

KEY PEOPLE   The topic of level of contact has occurred frequently throughout this book already. This is not surprising as it is probably the most difficult thing to get right in solution selling.

In any buying decision there tend to be the people who are doing the evaluation work, and those who will agree that the evaluation should happen and decide on the outcome.

While the selling team is bound to spend a lot of time with the evaluators, it is vital that it retains regular contact with the other group of decision-makers. This can be a political minefield. Most account managers have been told at some time or other that: "If you go above my head and sell to my boss I will make sure that you play no more part in this evaluation".

A variation on this is: "There is no purpose in your meeting the senior people, they will merely rubber-stamp my recommendation". In both of these cases someone, often the technical buyers, are acting as gatekeepers and preventing the selling team having access to decision-makers.

Once again the account manager needs to plan how he or she is going to prove the added value of having this access. You will not always succeed, but you have to try.

You need a statement from the top if you are going to understand the context of the proposed project. You need to hear the senior managers express their critical success factors in order to aim your proposal at the heart of the business.

It is important to use your senior management team well in this regard. Frequently a request for the two managing directors to meet will have the necessary effect of getting access for the account manager to a level otherwise denied.

Use such meetings well, and make sure that they promote the image and importance of the account manager, not the visiting senior manager. The next case is an example of this process going wrong.

EXAMPLE

Disaster at aerospace

I was introducing my managing director to the chairman of a major aerospace company. It was my MD's first visit to the chairman although not mine. I had met him on a few occasions, some business others more social.

In my briefing to my MD I had included all that I thought was significant in the account at that time, expressed the objectives of the meeting and noted the state of qualification of the two big sales campaigns which were current.

I had not included a problem which we were having in delivering a small but important component (let's call it the JF20) required in a project which was in mid-implementation. I did not include it because it never struck me that such a detail would arise at this level of meeting.

I had not allowed for the strategy and cunning of the IT director. I had warned him at the time of ordering that any delay on his part would result in my having difficulty in meeting his requirement for the JF20. The delay had occurred, and without tramping over my company's delivery priorities I could not achieve the optimum date for installation.

To be honest I wanted this slight inconvenience to happen so that the IT director would believe me the next time I told him that he needed to get on quickly with the ordering process. Nemesis was at hand.

Towards the end of what had until then been a very satisfactory meeting, the chairman produced an internal note from the IT director and said "I understand we need one of your JF20s to continue with one of our projects. He tells me that we are in the queue, but that the current forecast date is too late. Any chance we could jump the queue?"

My MD swallowed the bait in full. He asked for the use of a telephone and sent an instruction to get a JF20 on site within 24 hours. It was done and my credibility shattered.

My MD had at a stroke changed our effective level of contact from me, the account manager, to him, the managing director. From then on the IT director felt he had an open route of communication between the chairman and my MD whenever he wanted something non-standard or even just a favour. ○

In the qualification process the account manager needs to answer the following questions.

Do you know all the key people?

Even just making the initial list can be hazardous. In discussion with your main contact you should get fairly close to who is going to be involved. What you are looking for though, is who the decision-maker is going to turn to for an authoritative opinion on some aspect of the project.

The more people involved the harder the campaign. The higher the individuals in the organization, the more difficult it will be to get regular contact with them.

The definition of this question is: "Can we, when we need it, get access to anyone involved from the customer's side in the process of evaluation?" It is not good enough to have had them in the company box at Lord's, it must be the potential to meet them in a timely manner to discuss, probably among other things, this project.

> **The more people involved the harder the campaign.**

If the project is big enough or important enough to the buying company, this could be a lot of people. In one campaign which I will describe later, the selling team identified 50 people who would have some influence and involvement in the evaluation process.

Do we have as good access to the key people as your competitors do?

Another litmus test. In some cases you will not succeed in getting contact with all the people involved. This second test then becomes crucial. You are on a very uneven playing pitch if the competition is talking to people to whom you do not have access. If these people happen to be the most senior managers in the buying organization this could be critical to your hopes of success.

Finding the answer to this question is also tricky. Your contacts may not know that the competition has high-level contact, or they could choose not to give you that information. Probe deeply and use your sales instincts as well as your questioning technique.

If you remember my golden rule of qualification: "If a part of your campaign could be going wrong, it probably is" you will pay enough attention to competitive level of contact to ensure that you are not fighting the bidding battle with a considerable handicap.

Are they all informed of the pending buying decision?

As with all these qualification questions, this one is another effort to ensure that the customer is as committed as you to action. Having understood who will be involved in the decision-making process, the team now has to check that each and everyone is aware that a buying decision is planned.

In many instances where a sales team has insisted on involving all the key people early on, a sceptic or likely veto has been discovered.

Such a discovery does not necessarily mean that the campaign is over, it does mean that the team, probably with the help of someone in the customer, needs to make sure that such a person agrees to have an open mind.

The other point about speaking to all the key people early on is that you will detect their opening attitude to the proposed investment.

We will discuss later what is appropriate to be asking the different key people at the outset of a campaign. For the moment this question ensures that any key objector is discovered quickly.

TIMESCALE   If the key people question is one of the most important, then the timescale question is one of the most difficult to answer authoritatively. The human condition leads, in the main, to avoiding change and postponing decisions. A professional solution-seller is almost all the time proposing significant change and suggesting that a decision is made soon and urgently.

There is a conflict here which comes to a head when you are trying to tie someone down to a decision date. There is no magic answer.

If in the end a customer decides to postpone a decision or a project, that is their prerogative. All the salesperson can do is persistently probe for the feasibility of a decision and implementation date.

In pursuing the timescale question salespeople are also checking that the customer is actually in a position to buy. The credibility of a sales forecast depends on the degree to which the salesperson can convince his or her manager that the customer is realistically in a position to go ahead.

The first of two detailed questions is:

Have the key people agreed on a decision date?

Funnily enough this is more likely to be the case when a tender is in progress. If a customer goes out to a number of suppliers and requests a proposal or quotation, it is quite probable that at the same time they will give out a date for the proposals to be in, and at least by implication, a decision date.

It is more difficult to pin down a date during the early investigation phase. That is before the customer has arrived at that stage in the buying process we have called "select the necessary products and services and their suppliers".

It is also more difficult to get an agreed date where there is no competition involved, for example when additional functionality is being added to an existing service.

A thorough understanding of the customer's business processes will help with getting a secure answer to this question. If you know for example when the customer needs to get a recommendation ready to go to a particular Board meeting you will be in a position to predict to which meeting it could feasibly go.

If you are involved in the customer's return on investment process then this will be a further clue as to when a decision could be made.

In the end you ask the question of everyone you meet, and then ask them again when you meet them again. Listen hard to the manner in which the answer is given as well as the answer itself and you will detect the certainty or reliability of the response.

> **Ask the question early in the campaign.**

One more thing on this topic. Ask the question early in the campaign, for example at the first meeting. People are happier to take a commitment when the date of delivering it is a long way off. It is easier to get an agreed date in three months time, than to try and tie someone down to making a decision next week. Try to get the date agreed well in advance.

The second question is:

Is there an agreed implementation timescale?

However clever a product is and however much a customer needs it, the solution suggested by the product must be buyable and implementable.

I have discovered great opportunities for competitive edge when I was the first salesperson to work with the customer to produce the outline of an implementation plan.

I sometimes describe this as "timetable" selling. During the opening call with a prospect or customer on a particular campaign, a professional seller will try to get them to assist with the creation of a bar chart which identifies all the major milestones in the implementation of the proposed project.

Do not duck issues here. It is safer to talk about some difficult phase in the evaluation or implementation phase well in advance of the problem occurring.

The modification of this forms part of all subsequent calls and of course the requirement for a decision date to be part of the implementation plan is clear. There is an example of such a simple bar chart in Chapter 2, in the part concerned with the customer's establishment of implementation controls.

○ *Draw a bar chart of the implementation of one of your key products or services. Make sure you see it from the customer's point of view and that you cover all the required actions and milestones.*

FAST TRACK

SOLUTION So far the emphasis in the qualification process has been on buyability. We need now to turn to the sellability side. Account management is concerned with the long-term relationship with a customer, which in turn is concerned with delivering customer satisfaction time after time after time.

The proposed solution should have a number of attributes. First and foremost it must solve the problem or assist the customer to exploit the opportunity.

Next it must represent good business for the selling company. The main measures for this are profitability and risk.

The third attribute is nice-to-have rather than an essential. It is whether or not the project will lead to further business with the same customer and act as a reference to improve the chances of selling the solution to other prospects and customers.

The three subsidiary questions are:

Is your solution valid?

It is unlikely in a complex project that any solution offered will meet every single detail of the customer's specification. Most decisions of this nature have some compromise built in. The key for the selling team is to ensure the validity of its offering.

It must be a solution to the problem and give the benefits described in the customer assessment and business case. It must also fit in with the strategic policies and direction of the buying organization. Again these were identified in the customer assessment part of the planning process.

Given a positive response to these issues, the only other test of validity varies with every customer. Will they agree that the way you are suggesting is a valid answer to the problem?

Is the risk of your being able to deliver your promises acceptable?

An account manager may have a lot of internal selling to get a positive answer to this. In the section on organization we will look at a business process aimed at getting the agreement of all parties concerned, from the finance people to the engineers, that the risk is acceptable and fits into the selling company's strategy.

Is the project profitable now or through future sales?

Once again, this is often put into a business process whereby the account manager has to produce an estimated profit and loss account for the project.

The level of profit required will obviously vary project by project. At the most profitable end will be repeats of previous sales of high-value products while at the low end will be loss leaders where the whole reason for the sale is concerned with other sales which will flow from this one.

BASIS OF DECISION Establishing the basis of decision is said by many to be the key technique which separates the solution seller from the product salesperson or box shifter. It involves understanding from the customer's point of view all the issues surrounding the sale.

It is useful to break down the basis of decision, or BoD as I will call it, into three areas.

Financial basis of decision

In the section on finance at the start of the qualification checklist, we posed the question "Has the necessary return on investment process be completed?" The financial basis of decision is concerned with our finding out what that process is.

The account manager has to find an authoritative answer to the question "How do you as an organization do investment appraisal?"

> **The financial basis of decision is concerned with our finding out what that process is.**

Technical basis of decision

This part of the BoD tends to be the part on which most emphasis is placed. It is the statement by the company's technicians of the functionality that they require. It will go into great detail and be used as a template to compare the relative merits of each supplier's proposal.

Assuming that there are advantages and disadvantages for each proposal, the BoD will alter as different weightings are put on different functions. Indeed every technical presentation and demonstration is aimed at altering the basis of decision towards the unique features of the supplier making the presentation.

It is this ebb and flow in the BoD which these questions chart, and it is vital to use them frequently to measure progress.

Having said that, the technical BoD is by no means the only way that a customer will weigh up the merits of the bids on offer. It is the one into which the selling team will put a lot of effort and which can sometimes blind it to other issues which surround a complex decision.

Practical basis of decision

The third area which will dictate how a customer examines a project is its practicality. At this stage in the qualification process the team is trying to understand the ground rules.

What is important to the customer in terms of the impact on his people? Is the customer looking for ease of use or is minimum disruption of current processes during the implementation the key issue? Will the change be accepted willingly by the people concerned? And so on.

A further possible basis of decision on practicality grounds is organizational change. You may find management laying down a rule that no project will be entered into if it requires further organizational change.

This frequently occurs when the company has recently completed a big change for other reasons. Senior managers are aware that it is desirable to let an organization settle down from time to time.

The sub questions on BoD are as follows:

Have you agreed with the key people their criteria for deciding to go ahead?

Ask and keep asking, so that by the time it comes to making your proposal you can put it in their terms, not only from the business case point of view, but for all the key issues which surround the buying decision and the implementation.

Have you influenced this?

The professional account manager tries to get the customer to agree from his point of view the reasons why he will buy. This is much more powerful selling than just hitting them with features and benefits. The difference is between the following two statements:

"Aren't the people in the warehouse going to prefer to keep the same shelf layout even when the new system comes along?"

"If you buy the system I am selling you will not have to change the shelf layout."

The first is seeking to agree a criterion for or a BoD. The second is simply a statement of a feature.

As the campaign goes forward the basis of decision changes, and this question keeps reminding the selling team that it needs to make sure as far as it can that the current criterion suits its case.

In the end, of course, the BoD, which includes a feature or issue that is unique to one of the selling companies, tilts the balance firmly in their favour.

IMPLEMENTABILITY This word is coined to allow the selling team to assess how well it is organized to ensure an efficient implementation. It examines the resource requirement which will result in a successful project from both sides point of view.

There are three sub questions:

Are the customer's implementation resources available and allocated to this project?

Once again the professional solution seller is being up front with what the customer is going to have to do. A resource deficiency or skill absence should offer opportunity to the seller rather than a threat.

> **A resource deficiency or skill absence should offer opportunity.**

Do you have management agreement to the sales resources required to carry out the campaign plan?

At the first planning session the answer to this will be "No". It is not until the team has presented the plan and its resource implications to management and got their agreement to their allocation that this question becomes positive.

Are the implementation support resources from your side identified and allocated?

If you are to be convincing in your presentation of how the project will succeed if the buyer says "Yes", you need to know that the support will be available at the time it will be needed.

The risk which your company will take by making this sale is to a considerable extent defined by understanding what support will be necessary and having a very good idea of where it is coming from.

This question is rarely simple. Management estimate resource requirements from a knowledge base which is inevitably incomplete. They are making their best estimates not only of resource requirements but also of what projects and combinations of projects are actually going to be sold and implemented.

COMPETITIVE POSITION

All the qualification work which has gone before should allow the team to answer the crucial question of whether or not it is likely to win this business against the competition.

The biggest waste of any salesperson's time is the time he or she spends on bids and tenders which are then lost. At the end this is what qualification is about: "Am I spending my own and my team's time wisely? Is there anywhere else that this time could be more profitably used?"

There are two sub questions:

Can you identify one or more areas where you have competitive advantage?

Without this the team is selling on price. That is, if all other things are equal, the buying team will choose the cheapest bid. This is an unacceptable situation and the selling team must try to establish some feature of its offering which distinguishes it from the competition.

Risk is a good area. Look at your company, its experience, size, etc and try to get the customer to understand how much more likely the project is to be successful if they go with you.

Whatever the area, find your competitive edge, so that in the action plan part of the campaign planning process you can work out how to exploit that edge.

Is there an acceptably small number of competitors bidding?

Some buying companies start off the market testing and bidding process by inviting everyone who could possibly be involved to give information and presentations.

There is a lot of risk in this for the selling teams who could get too deeply embroiled in selling before the project has sufficient definition. They need to assess whether or not the project represents a good business opportunity for them.

This question will make the team limit its effort and lay a plan to try as quickly as possible to get the competing teams whittled down to an acceptable level.

drawing the spider's web

It is very useful to present the qualification checklist as a radar diagram which, because of its appearance, I call the *spider's web* (see Figure 7.1).

In time planning teams will start to see patterns in their spider's webs which they can recognize. You can also use the spider's web as a presentation aid when describing the state of a sales campaign to a manager or other interested party.

Some companies have put the spider's web into their culture. They have familiarized everyone with the concept so that there is a completely consistent approach to qualification and briefings.

Fig 7.1

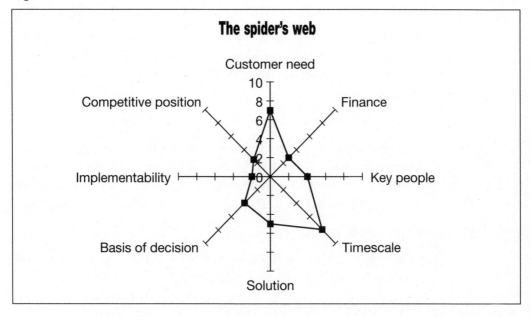

The rationale looks like this:

Customer need (score 7)

There is a good *prima facie* requirement which is agreed by the decision-maker to be strategically desirable. It will be well worth our effort. The only problem here is that we do not understand the process for deciding on return on investment.

Finance (score 3)

The decision-maker has said that he will make the money available, if his people come to him with a business case. It is not in a budget yet.

Key people (score 4)

We know who the key people are, but have no further access to the decision-maker until the time of proposal. The technical recommender who is taking the lead, is trying to block us from the user recommenders.

Timescale (score 8)

Good news here as the timescale is driven by a product launch which the customer is planning as a key date. The pressure on the launch date comes from legislation, so it is highly unlikely to be postponed.

Solution (score 5)

We have done this sort of thing many times before, but we are going to have to work with a third party with whom we have had no dealings. Once we agree the way ahead with the third party, the situation should improve.

Basis of decision (score 4)

We do not know the financial basis of decision. The technical basis is clear but contains no unique reason why they should buy from us. Our lack of contact with the user recommenders means that we do not understand the practical issues to be covered.

Implementability (score 3)

It is a bit early in the campaign to be able to allocate resources. On the face of it, it does not look too difficult.

Competitive position (score 2.5)

There are four competitors bidding and we have no reason to think that we are better or worse placed than any other.

FAST TRACK

○ *Complete the qualification checklist for the campaign you have in mind.*

○ *From your feelings about the campaign draw up a spider's web.*

8

planning winning sales campaigns - 4

selling the business case to the key people

People buy from people. The next analysis concerns the key people, their attitudes at the start of the campaign and their inter-relationships. It's time to plan what you are going to say to each individual involved.

who is involved and what is their role?

You need first to draw a chart of the people who will exert influence in some way on the buying decision.

EXAMPLE

Who makes decisions for the holiday company?

A package holiday company is considering a proposal to review its entire communications network. Because the decision will dramatically change a vital interface to the company's market, the following key people will have a strong say in any decision:

● The managing director.

● The marketing director.

● The sales director.

● The IT director.

● The business development manager.

● The financial controller.

The following is an example organization chart.

Fig 8.1

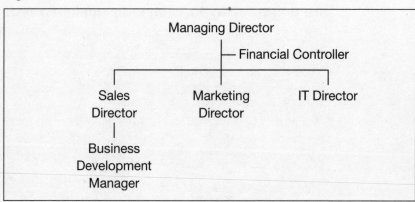

The selling team will now try to define the opening situation as it meets the key people early in the campaign. The first issue is to try to understand the person's role in the decision-making process.

○ *Draw the organization chart of the key people in the campaign you are planning.*

It is useful and practical to consider four possibilities.

Understand the person's role in the decision-making process.

● Decision-maker.
● User recommender.
● Technical recommender.
● Champion.

We will take them in turn.

DECISION-MAKER In any basic selling course, the instructor will, quite rightly, tell the delegates that they must spend time assessing and deciding who is the final decision-maker. In practice this is more difficult than it sounds.

On more than one occasion I have taken large orders, and after the campaign still been unsure as to who was the decision-maker. Companies take most complex decisions after considerable discussion and authority can move as the campaign progresses.

I have also seen it from the other point of view.

EXAMPLE

I was not sure who made the decision and I was one of the key people

When I was a director of a small company with five directors, the Board made a decision to buy a computer. I watched the process with keen interest, as I knew that I would discover new aspects of selling from the buyer's point of view.

Naturally, when the salespeople came to meet me they asked the question "Who will make the final decision?" To begin with I was convinced that the managing director would dominate the decision as he did most things.

Later in the campaign I became less sure. The managing director appeared to me to be losing interest and another director was working closely with the technical person.

In the end all parties on the Board agreed and once again I could not, hand on heart, say who I thought answered the description "decision maker". ○

Despite this experience we can attribute certain rules as to who is the decision-maker. The decision-maker:

- Gives the final go ahead. Because of this, the decision-maker is frequently the most senior person involved. If that most senior person does not make the decision, then he or she will have the ability in any case to veto the project.

- Has direct access to money. The budget may be delegated, but the decision-maker will have the ability to spend. Notice that this is rarely a finance person who is more likely to advise the decision-maker on, for example, the return on investment of the project.

- Is one person. No corporation is a democracy. In the end there are a limited number of people who will make the key decisions.

- Puts the emphasis on the bottom line. When you spend a company's money, you take responsibility for the good use of that capital. It is a very competitive world and one manager is continuously trying to convince others that he or she will make the best use of funds. Thus the emphasis of the spender is "What will this do for the business?" not "How elegant a solution is this?"

- Is highly concerned with organizational change. As we saw in the section on how a sensible person plans to buy and implement technology, there is one certainty. If you change how a business process works then your people are going to have to change how they do their jobs. Decision-makers and other senior people in organizations are acutely aware of this. They will look carefully at proposals to satisfy themselves that the organization and its people can handle the change, accept and implement it. "Will it work here?" is the key question they will ask.

- Checks the strategic relevance of the proposal. Also as we saw in Chapter 2, senior people will always question whether or not a new proposal follows the strategy the Board has mapped for the company.

This checklist not only helps the team to decide who the decision-maker is, it also helps them to define what topics they need to discuss with him or her.

The next category of buying influencer is the user recommender. Taking a simple view, the user recommender almost certainly is in a line job, not a staff one. Fundamentally it is line managers who make a company's products and sell them profitably. They in effect run the business.

No matter how significant a technical or financial recommender may look in the buying process, the line managers are going to have their say. If the project will impact on their performance and performance measures, they will have significant parts to play in estimating how the new idea will affect the business.

EXAMPLE

IT people do not estimate the impact of a new project on the holiday business

In the holiday company example, it is obvious that the IT director will have a lot of influence. He or she knows the current situation and salespeople will have to convince them that the telecommunications strategy they propose will meet the company's requirements.

But the cost justification will come through the amount of improvement they can expect in, for example, management productivity and increased market share. Only the sales and marketing directors can assess on the company's behalf what that improvement is likely to be.

The IT director can authoritatively say whether the technology will do the job, he cannot predict what impact the new environment will have on the business's revenues and profits. ○

Here are the clues as to whether a key person belongs in the category "user recommender". The user recommender:

● **Owns the benefits. When a business case is made for a recommended course of action it affects the job evaluation of the user recommender. The benefits which formed part of the business case become management objectives once the decision to invest is made.**

A similar situation in FMCG

The buyers and buying controllers in a large retail organization will make recommendations on the promotion of particular categories of products they believe the stores can sell.

Once the Board backs an advertising campaign, for example, it will then monitor the sales of the product during the following period. If the sales director was also involved then this group would represent the user recommenders in the decision-making process. ○

This connection between the estimating of benefits and setting of management objectives helps us to understand why managers are conservative when they look at new business cases.

User recommenders want to make low risk estimates of benefits

The production director of the glass company mentioned in Chapter 2 had to assist with the estimating of benefits by saying how many people he believed would be saved on the production lines due to the new instrumentation.

His starting point was that he had no doubt that they would save four people. He thought there was a reasonable chance that the saving would be eight, and he speculated that if all went really well, they might save 16.

When the project manager asked for the production director's agreement to be quoted in the proposal, he would only agree to the lowest estimate of four people.

He knew that if the project went ahead, his budget and headcount would be cut by the number of people declared in the proposal. ○

- Manages the application of the project. The line management of an organization are responsible for the people who will use the equipment or sell FMCGs. The telecommunications manager may be responsible for providing the hardware and software of the new network, but it is the people in the sales offices who will use the new facilities and make more sales.

- Is often numerous. All the store managers will take responsibility for selling the new product. Each and every sales manager will take a higher sales target as a result of implementing a

Choosing a sample at both ends of the spectrum

A company has a network of 10 outlets selling tyres and exhausts. Head office management took a decision to computerize in a much more sophisticated way the methods used to control stock.

The project team included the sales director who could see that better stock control would lead to fewer stockouts. This would in turn lead to better customer satisfaction, and in the end higher sales.

The profit element of these higher sales was a major element of the business case.

The sales director is plainly a user recommender. But the persons who actually make the sales are the depot managers in the field. A wise selling team will certainly go and look at how the depot managers operate. The team will want to tune its proposition to accord with what the depot managers find acceptable.

The team may not need to see all 10 but it needs a sample. Personally in that case I would visit two. I would get the sales director to suggest one manager who will probably welcome the new methods, and one who will, in all probability, resist them to the death. That way I know how to sell the Board on getting the line managers committed to the project.

project aimed at higher sales. The selling team is going to have to decide how many user recommenders it is necessary to see. Often a top level contact and then a representative sample is what is required.

- Is close to the users involved in the new way of doing things. They are probably the managers of the people who are accepting change. They will therefore feel their success or pain.

Decide how many user recommenders it is necessary to see.

- Puts emphasis on making it happen. They will look closely at the implementation plan including familiarization and training.

This brings us to the next role of key people in the buying process – technical recommenders.

TECHNICAL RECOMMENDER These people are particularly important if the product or service in question has a high level of technical complexity. A billboard advertising campaign will require less technical know-how than one which involves multi-media or broadcast fax. They come in two identifiable groups – financial and technical expertise.

Financial expertise is normally concerned with the company's rules on return on investment or budgeting. The technical expertise normally concerns the complex detail of the project under consideration.

The big danger with technical recommenders is that they will soak up the time of the selling team in discussing the detail of the technical solution, and by so doing keep the team away from the user recommenders and decision-maker who are likely to be more influential in the final decision.

The role of a technical recommender is often self-created and tend to have the following attributes. The technical recommenders:

- Are often very numerous. In the case of technology the senior technical people frequently call in many of their staff who have knowledge or interest in a particular topic. Indeed quite often a sales campaign has as its starting point an inquiry by a technical person who has picked up information about a product from a technical magazine. This can be a very useful entry point, but requires strict qualification to make sure that the opportunity is real.

- Assess the measurable and quantifiable. Having probably little knowledge of the company's business situation, they tend to concentrate on what it is possible to measure. This gives them on the one hand the ability to advise management on whether or not a particular product has enough power or features to do the job. On the other hand, unless prompted by the selling team or by the user recommenders, they may miss out other considerations concerned with the practicality of implementation.

- Are often barriers to getting to the other key people. Seeing the buying decision as their issue, they can feel threatened by a selling team proposing to talk to the users and decision-maker. At best "Talk to them if you like but it will have no impact on who gets the business". At worst "Talk to my bosses and I will cut your throat". This is a big topic and one which is properly dealt with in basic selling, but the fundamental technique is simple to state. You have to show the technical recommenders that it is in their interests as well for the selling team to have access to the other key people. When we come to account planning we will look at the general level of contact problem more closely.

TRICKS OF THE TRADE

Competitive selling in complex situations

A team selling to a bank had a particular problem with a senior manager who took this gatekeeping role very seriously. She regarded the decision as hers and any suggestion that anyone else would be involved as a slight on her professionalism.

The selling team found in the qualification process that it could not understand the real need or the cost justification without meeting some of the senior bankers.

During the campaign planning session dealing with the people issues, someone asked the key question: "When does she go on holiday?" The team found out and during her holiday made the necessary contacts. On her return it had to make a good case to her for what it had done. The team had done it, however, and got the required information and invitations to return.

The account manager and selling team had proved two essential rules of competitive selling in complex situations:

1. It is easier to ask for forgiveness rather than permission. It is frequently better not to ask the gatekeeper if you may talk to others. If they then say no, you have a bigger problem after the meeting than if you never asked in the first place.

2. When you are right, you have some might even when you are in the position of prospective supplier. If it is true that you cannot make a proper presentation without speaking to the line management team, then doing so will eventually be seen to be in order.

> **It is easier to ask for forgiveness rather than permission.**

● Concentrate on things you cannot do. This is one of the reasons that technical recommenders can take up so much of your time. They force you into heavy internal selling in your own organization. They coerce you into meeting a technical requirement which may seem important technically but actually has little impact on the main thrust of your proposal. Their discovery of an alternative product which is "three key strokes better" than yours can lead to an element of blindness about the complete picture.

- Often say no. In a complex sale there are rarely times when one supplier has got the lead in every aspect of the proposal. Technical recommenders are quick to point that out and say no to the technical solution even though the business solution is strong.

Technical recommenders place an emphasis on meeting specifications. They are quite rightly looking for first class products and services. From their company's point of view they are also in the implementation phase responsible for customer satisfaction.

In the end they carry the can as to whether the money spent has given the buying company what it wanted and needed. They are in all respects important people in the decision-making process.

CHAMPION

Any person in the decision-making process can combine one of the roles above with another, that of your champion. "Inside salesperson" is another term used to describe a person who is attracted by your proposition and takes an interest in your developing the ability to build a winning case.

The champion is like a torch to a selling team as they peer into the darkness of the buying organization's politics. It is difficult to win a major sales campaign without the assistance of someone on the inside.

Here's what the champion can do once the team have him or her in a supportive frame of mind:

- Provide information. This information will include the internal politics of the organization. It will contain the data required by the team to recognize where power and influence really lie.

- Help with the selling. If the champion is convinced of the merit of a case, it is often more powerful for him or her to present the case to the key people. When a salesperson claims a benefit the people listening are likely to dilute the strength of the message because of the position of the messenger. If, however, one of their own is saying the same thing it can be more compelling.

TRICKS OF
THE TRADE

Using a champion to handle price objections

A price objection is the nightmare scenario of most salespeople. Unless an account manager has added value considerably in the buying process, he or she is going to be vulnerable to a cheaper competitor.

With a user recommender or a champion, classic price objection technique goes like this:

Recommender: "You have a problem on price, frankly. Whatever the merits and demerits of the case, and goodness knows they are difficult enough to tie down, you are more expensive than both your competitors."

Account manager: "If we were the same price or cheaper, would you buy from us?" (Incidentally this technique crashes at this point if the account manager cannot keep silent.) If he or she does, there is generally a pause and then the recommender will come up with the objections to your proposal. This is very useful.

Alternatively the recommender may say "Yes." In this case simply ask "Why?" and then sit back while the buyer persuades him or herself to buy the most expensive product. It can be somewhat hilarious to watch this technique in a car showroom.

Only use this technique in a buying department if you have your champion with you. If you ask the question "Would you buy from us if we were the same price?" to professional buyers they will probably simply say "No".

If, however, you have your champion with you, he or she can explain to the buyer the added benefits or reduced risk if they buy from you. It is much more persuasive coming from an insider.

● Get you in to see the right people. While senior managers may be sceptical about the relevance and value of meeting a salesperson, they are less likely to be dismissive of a request coming from a respected person in their company.

WATCH OUT!

Do not put your money on a loser

Another grave danger is developing champions. Notice that your hero has to have real credibility with the management team who are colleagues. The opposite and you have an inside suicide kit rather than an inside salesman.

I have witnessed a situation where a managing director included a technical recommender in a project team simply so as not to cause the person concerned to lose face. In fact the MD considered the person out of touch, and any recommendation coming from him would be as likely to push the MD in the opposite direction.

Pity the selling teams who regarded such a person as a potential champion.

The line of respect is therefore that the champion has respect for you and your company and the buying company has respect for the champion.

As champions become more committed, so their emphasis becomes more and more on getting success from the campaign and its implementation.

EXAMPLE

Management roles in the holiday company

It is likely that the managing director will be the decision-maker. It is almost certain that the sales and marketing directors are user recommenders. It is also almost certain that the IT director and financial controller are technical recommenders.

The position of the business development manager is harder to gauge, and the account manager will have to keep an open mind on this until he or she gets inside the company. ○

FAST TRACK

○ *Take the key people you identified previously in the organization chart.*

○ *Assign to each the role you believe they will have in the decision-making process.*

when do you want to meet the key people?

The selling team now moves on to the next key issue of timing. It is vital that it meets the key people at a time in the campaign when it has something sensible to ask or say.

If the account manager is going to get the level of the sales calls right, he or she has to be in the right place at the right time.

It is helpful in this regard to define the selling cycle in a serial way, much as we defined the buying cycle earlier on. The team can then examine what information it wants from whom and produce a call plan.

I will take the following as being the various stages of the selling cycle and examine each one separately:

- **Make the approach.**

- **Establish need.**

- **Basis of decision.**

- **Build the business case.**

- **Demonstration and reference visits.**

- **Propose.**

- **Close.**

As with the buying cycle, life is not serial like this, and things will be happening simultaneously with different members of the key buyers.

MAKE THE APPROACH

There are two schools of thought on the level at which a salesperson should make an approach into a new subsidiary or division of an existing key account.

The first method involves sending letters and getting in at the highest level possible.

The second starts with the people most involved with the type of product or service which the seller sells. The argument goes: "Before I meet with the managing director, I need to get a briefing about the current situation from the people most involved."

This second method leads people who sell **| "Go in at the top".** training products into the personnel department, FMCG salespeople into the buyers and computer salespeople into the computer department.

The reality unfortunately is that the correct method depends on a number of questions. Let us take the "Go in at the top" way first.

There is really only one potential danger in this approach, and that is that if the call does not go well you have given yourself a severe disadvantage in all subsequent dealings with the account.

Having said that, it is not difficult to make a high-level approach if you do some research work on published material and go in with a series of intelligent open questions.

EXAMPLE

Using the power of a high-level contact

As a sales trainee, I took an inactive part in a call on the chairman of a multinational conglomerate of diversified industries. I was there to learn from the senior key account manager who was making the call.

I learned during the call, but not as much as I learned in subsequent meetings with other executives in the organization.

I was at a meeting subsequently with the managing director of a small subsidiary within the group and innocently mentioned that I had met the chairman recently. The result was electric. "You met the chairman?" "Er yes." "Did he mention my business?"

I was very impressed with the difference the meeting had on my image and standing within the account. As a result I have leaned towards the high level side of the argument ever since.

Of course it does not always work out quite so well. I once made a call on the general manager of a factory which belonged to a subsidiary of a large food processing company. At the time I was working for a company called ICL and I had made the appointment by telephone.

On arrival I introduced myself and he asked me to repeat the name of my company. When the manager heard this he said:"Oh, I thought you were from ICI. If I had known the truth I would never have seen you".

I never recovered from this. He remained highly suspicious of me despite the fact that it had been a complete misunderstanding and I had been the innocent party. ○

The advantages of going in high are legion. It means that when you start talking at lower levels in the organization you can use the high level call to set the tone of the new relationship.

The only reason for going in at a lower level which makes complete sense is where an executive of another company in the group introduces you. In this case you go in at the level of introduction and try to keep the options open for a higher level of contact during the meeting.

Of course, in reality it can be impossible to get agreement to a meeting at this stage in the relationship with the account and you will have to settle for less. We have a tendency though to imagine that this is always the case and not try for the alternative.

If you are comfortable to go in to senior management and make a good call with limited knowledge of the business then do it. If you are not comfortable, work on it.

It is a very necessary skill of the professional account manager to be able to handle business meetings at all levels. Indeed some would say it is the litmus test to be able to call on general managers without having to give them great presentations on your products and services. If you tend to use a brochure with senior people you are almost certainly getting the level wrong.

ESTABLISH NEED The requirement to understand the business need, or the opportunity which your offerings bring to the prospective customer has to be the first significant hurdle from both parties' point of view.

However clever the product, however brilliant the technology, the buying company has to discover the relevance to its strategy and an area of the business which will show improvement if the sale goes ahead.

It is in the buyer's interest therefore that this discovery happens as soon as possible. They do not want to waste time either.

From the selling team's point of view it is vital to find the *prima facie* reason for buying early in the campaign. It is of no help to spend a lot of time demonstrating and selling if the project is subsequently vetoed by the user recommenders because they do not see the business issues involved.

Misled by joint enthusiasm

This is a particular problem with new technology. The salespeople for Dialcard will have little trouble gaining the interest of the technology people and even of the marketing people who will see all sorts of possible uses for the new product.

The problem is in the phrase "all sorts of uses." If the salesperson cannot tie down a particular application then he or she is going to end up in the classic position of a low priority idea for which there is no powerful backing.

What happens is that the salesperson delivers a demonstration card which the interested executive passes round a number of colleagues. They phone the salesperson and he or she answers queries, and gets more excited about the prospects in the company. Time and expense continue to drain away.

Eventually the enthusiasm starts to die. No-one has said "I want the card for this" but no-one has said "We do not want to go ahead." Finally the clients stop calling the salesperson back and a hot prospect comes off the forecast sheet.

From this and what has gone above in terms of people's role in the decision-making process, it becomes obvious that the key people at the established need stage are the decision-maker and the user recommenders. After all the latter "own the benefits" and are the people who will be responsible for producing the improvements if implementation takes place.

> **The key people at the established need stage are the decision-maker and the user recommenders.**

I like to establish a "potential pot of gold" early in the process. By this I mean that I like to agree with a user recommender that there is scope for a major pay back if the project went ahead.

Good open questions which at the early stage of a campaign carry little threat are the right weapons:

Remember, it is easier for user recommenders to believe in a global benefit at this time in the campaign. They know it will be some time, and they will have much more evidence, before they are required to put the detailed numbers together.

In terms of timing therefore, it is likely that the selling team will plan to meet the user recommenders very early in the campaign to complete the vital task of establishing need.

BASIS OF DECISION

We have seen a number of ways of distinguishing product selling from key account and solution selling. Basis of decision is another.

In professional solution selling the salesperson tries to get into the shoes of the prospective buyer and understand from their angle under what circumstances a sensible business person would take a positive decision.

It is useful to divide the basis of decision into three parts. There is a financial, technical and practical basis of decision.

The financial basis of decision is frequently a set of rules. Those rules are generally in the remit of the finance department.

The selling team will plan, therefore, to see the finance people at a stage in the campaign when there is a sufficient *prima facie* business case to suggest that this idea could become a project. It follows that the need must be established and agreed before it is necessary to check on the financial basis of decision.

A technical recommender cuts through the political fog

A sales team was struggling with the politics of an organization. The management team in the buying company seemed divided and to have overlapping roles.

The team found it very difficult to decide who would really be influential in the buying decision.

A visit to the financial controller was the key activity. The account manager asked how the financial case would be made and what the financial basis of decision was. The response made a lot of things clear.

The financial controller simply told the account manager how he would assemble the cost benefit analysis. He explained that he would rely on Mr X and Ms Y for the costs of the project. If they were agreed that the costs had been well estimated then they would be the numbers which would go into the analysis.

He further explained that although Mr X and Ms Y would probably also comment on the benefits side of the calculation, that would carry little weight with the finance department.

For the income stream or benefit case the financial controller would listen to Messrs A and B. He also said that he thought Mr A would give the more positive view of the matter, with Mr B more conservative. This helped the financial controller to gauge the risk of the project.

This information was as gold to the selling team members. They not only understood the financial basis of decision, payback within two years, but they had new information or confirmation of the role of the key people in the decision.

They could now update that part of the plan with increased confidence. ○

There was another interesting facet to this story of a technical recommender dealing with roles. During the sales call the account manager needed to make almost no reference to the detail of the project itself.

By sticking with the right question the team had planned the level of the call correctly. It also gained the respect of a finance person by talking about topics which were interesting and within his authority.

In this context the finance department looks like a technical recommender. Basically it will advise the decision maker whether or not the cost benefit analysis achieves the company's aims.

The technical basis of decision comes next. Most selling teams put a lot of effort into this part of the process. They are anxious to agree with the technicians what features are important in the proposal they are about to make.

They are also, quite rightly, anxious to get some recognition that the uniques of their products and services should be regarded as an important decision criterion. After all, if there is a feature which is crucial to the basis of decision, and you are the only team who could supply it, then you should win.

As for timing, it is clear that the technical basis of decision should be established after the need and after the financial criteria are agreed. In reality, teams often get involved with the technicalities too early in the campaign and spend too much time on the subject.

It is likely that the technical basis of decision will be the prerogative of the technical recommenders.

Equally important is the practical basis of decision. This concerns both the user recommenders and the technical recommenders.

Once again, if the selling team is really in the shoes of the buying company, then discussion about how the project will be implemented will take place once the need is agreed and the business case understood at least in outline.

Examples of the concerns which the buyers will have are:

- **Will the people concerned with changing their jobs be happy to do so?**

- **How much disruption will there be during any changeover?**

- **How much technical risk are we prepared to take?**

- **Will there be any knock-on problems in other areas caused by the change?**

- **How long will the solution last before technology or other changes such as market differences make it out of date?**

The key here in all discussions of basis of decision is to pre-empt objections. Rather than come across concerns when the proposal has been written **| Pre-empt objections.** and presented, the selling team uses professional questions to establish what is important to the customer in judging the proposal.

While the senior user recommenders will give you an overview of the business case, you need now to recognize the detail of the cost benefit case. The people involved in this may not be part of the key buying group, but often work for them.

There can be great sensitivities here, particularly if the people concerned are worried about technology or other changes costing their jobs.

Your champion should be able to help with this. He or she will direct you towards the people who will co-operate and be easily motivated into assisting with the production of the business case.

Do not underestimate the help which the finance department can give in sorting the numbers out into a concise report.

**TRICKS OF
THE TRADE**

Getting the help of an accountant to get to the business case

In the very complex sales campaign concerned with the review of the telecommunications network of the holiday company we have been following, the financial controller came up trumps for the team again when he insisted that all the applications were reduced to a simple flip chart.

He demanded that against each of the application areas the team gave him the capital costs, the running costs year on year, the one-off savings and the annual benefits.

Against each of these he then mapped the executives he would turn to as authoritative opinions on each and every figure. The team and he then went through each item and noted a figure or the agreement of the person concerned in each box.

By this method the team was able easily to identify where the holes in the business case formation were.

In this part of the planning process the team has now decided when it intends to meet each of the key buyers. It is likely that the plan will entail meeting all of the senior people involved by this time in the selling cycle. What comes next is the involvement of others who will influence the influencers.

FAST TRACK

○ *Against your list of key people, note when you would like to get the key people involved.*

○ *If you are already into the campaign compare what actually happened with how you would plan it now given the arguments above.*

Try to make these as telling as possible. Tailor them as much as possible to the actual requirement of this campaign. It does not take much to turn a general demonstration into something which looks more or less prepared for a particular customer.

Reference visits should try to match levels. Do not take the IT manager to see the managing director of the reference customer. This produces the psychological impact that the visiting company is senior to the reference.

In general, sellers mistime demonstrations by holding them too early. If you have not got near agreement on the items above in the selling cycle list, try to avoid being dragooned into a demonstration. Simply, you cannot tailor the visit to the customer until you are thoroughly aware of the need and the basis of decision.

All the time you are trying to pre-empt objections and sell benefits which are completely right for this customer. Do not spoil that by going off at half cock in the "dem".

PROPOSE

There is a frequent danger that the next time you meet the decision maker after your preliminary meeting is when you present your proposal. This means that in many cases you are making a proposal which disobeys good selling technique.

In an ideal world each significant item of the proposal should be agreed with the appropriate member of the buying team before you formally propose. Once again the tendency is to make the proposal too early, sometimes very much too early.

If proposals contain elements of surprise, it tends to elongate the selling process. Hold back on the proposal until you are pretty certain that you are in a position when it is at least possible if not likely that the customer is going to accept it.

> **The tendency is to make the proposal too early.**

The difference between a quotation and a proposal is this. A seller sends a quotation at any time in a sales campaign probably at the behest of the buyer. An account manager sends a proposal to confirm the agreements he or she has made with the key people in the buying process.

To summarize on timing proposals, it is generally disadvantageous to arrange to meet a key person at the proposal stage of the buying cycle. Try to get at least a short meeting with everyone beforehand.

CLOSE

A similar position occurs at the close. It is undesirable, if I am afraid not unusual, to meet key people for the first time at a meeting where you are hoping to take the order. All the issues concerning proposals are also relevant here.

However, it is not unusual. The decision-maker may very well wish to meet the selling team or account manager at the time when all that is left is to sign the contract.

It is a difficult meeting to prepare, since it is likely that all the key people will be present. If the selling team has run the campaign well, then it will have been careful to talk to each individual at the right level and in the appropriate terms.

It is logically impossible to do this when you are dealing with a committee. Probably the best answer is to pitch the presentation at the level right for the decision-maker and try to avoid going down detailed discussion routes particularly with the technical recommenders.

EXAMPLE

I was mugged by politicians

Probably the most disastrous closing presentation I ever made was to the sub-committee of the finance committee of a large local authority. Three companies were bidding to replace and expand a considerable amount of computer equipment.

I decided to take with me a very sales-oriented technician in case the IT manager, an officer who would also be there as an adviser to the committee, asked reasonable questions which were beyond me.

I also took along a senior sales manager whom I had briefed carefully. He prepared a good script which I vetted. Rather ominously he also warned me that he was a lousy presenter. I ignored this remark on two grounds. He was a very good communicator in meetings and sales calls, and I did not think it was possible to get a senior sales job without being at least competent on one's feet.

We opened with the sales manager who froze and stumbled and stammered through the text we had agreed, but managing at the same time to make it more or less impossible to understand.

▶

You could feel as well as see the restlessness of the councillors, themselves obviously reasonable orators, and the embarrassment of the IT manager who felt a little responsible for what he was putting his masters through.

The chairman was a most fair and calm person who kept the questioning to a minimum at that stage and we passed on to the next presentation. I gave a short history of our joint success in implementing computer systems with solid benefits to all concerned. I then passed on to the overview of our new proposal and tried to demonstrate our competitive advantages in terms of the agreed basis of decision.

By now I would not say we were a wow, but we had recovered to at least looking professional. In retrospect I should have asked for the order at that time. Or at least I should have asked what we still needed to do to get the order.

However, I had brought the technician with me and he had prepared a short, but quite interesting, few words about a technical innovation which distinguished our offering from the competition's. I overcame my instincts and put him on.

All went well until the IT manager asked a question which the techie handled quickly and well. He had to drop into some detail but it was short and sweet. A Labour councillor then asked another question which was at a high level. The technician misunderstood the level and proceeded into a detailed explanation which was much more than the questioner required.

The politicians at this stage finally got bored, and did what they do when they are bored – had a snipe at the opposing party. The snipe received a firm retort followed by a shouted list of mistakes the ruling party had made in several years of office.

By now the conversation was a million miles away from the topic in question and I looked to the chairman to help us out. He tried manfully, but when politicians smell fear or blood they go for the jugular. The chairman lost control and pandemonium broke out. It was like Prime Minister's Question Time on a bad day.

Our closing opportunity ended in chaos and the association of ideas which the committee had with my company was malevolence and boredom. Needless to say we did not win the business. ○

Lessons to be learned from the experience:

1. Always believe people who say they are bad at presenting.

2. Try not to meet people for the first time at closing presentations.

3. Do not risk answering any technical points with laymen present.

4. Keep presentations to politicians short and high level.

FAST TRACK

○ *Add to your key people chart the timing which would be most suitable for your campaign.*

what is their attitude at the beginning of the selling process?

In getting people to adopt your suggestions and proposals you have to be perceptive and methodical. My colleague John Wright was responsible for the development of a planning strategy for selling to the key people based on the principle of change management.

You have to be perceptive and methodical.

As you consider the actions you need to take with each of the buyer's people, consider their starting point and attitude towards the change you are proposing. In your initial meeting with them they will reveal how they feel about the issue and how comfortable they will be about changing how they or their people do things.

Plot this starting point against the list in column 1 of the following table. The list looks like this:

● **Antagonistic** means that for some reason they do not like even the thought of what you are proposing.

● **Indifferent** means that they do not see at the moment what is in it for them or unaware that there will be an impact on them.

● **Aware** means that they know of the proposal but have little knowledge about its impact on them.

- **Interested** means that they have got to the stage of weighing the matter up and considering it a possibility.

- **Trying-out mentally** is a very good sign. It means that the person is trying to work out how things will be for him or her if the proposal wins support. Perhaps the most famous example of trying-out mentally is the couple considering buying a house. When they discuss where they would put different pieces of furniture, they are at this stage.

- **Trying** it has them simulating the proposal in their own environment.

- **Committed** is the stage to which you are trying to get as many of the key people as possible as quickly as possible. Once there is a moment in time when they are all committed, ask for the order.

- **Internalizes** denotes the time when the buyers have accepted the change and the new situation is now the norm.

As we move towards action planning in the team planning process the table below should help you to decide which category each of the key people is in and therefore the approach you should take.

Let this adoption strategy be your guide and consider at least those actions relevant to the stage your buyer is at.

Key strategies for key people

A basic checklist

Levels of support	Signs	Your role	Possible actions
Antagonistic	Rude, irrational, objects. No time for you. "We already do something like it" "Yes, but"	Be pleasant and tolerant. Bide your time to scatter seed corn	Be welcoming, smile, talk about your interests. Go at their pace. Use their names. Reduce any threat situation. Remove any fear or anxiety
Indifferent	Shows no real interest. Changes the subject. Introduces red herrings, fidgets	As above	Approach and be approachable. Reward approximations to awareness and interest in solution or related topics. Face to face is best here but use of the telephone, letter, article or cassette through post followed up soon afterwards can be useful. Do not forget use of recommenders or champions
Aware	Passive. Has little information. Does not look for information. Has no opinions	Presenter	Look for openings and established need. Listen for any expression of need. Obtain attention by appealing to these needs, keeping presentation of solution brief and focused on need. Use oral, written and pictorial material for them to read or look at. Discuss with them later

Levels of support	Signs	Your role	Possible actions
Interested	Open mind. Seeks information. Begins to form opinions. Personal concerns and questions about how the innovation will affect them and their organization	Counsellor/ consultant	Match need to solution. Match information and characteristics of solution to real needs and basis of decision. Involve them in discussing and encourage ideas from them. Link with the job and environment. Identify personal concerns, "their win", answer questions and provide information
Trying out mentally	Mentally tries out. Imagines in own situation. Expresses some views. Decides if worth trying	Demonstrator	Present and describe solution in more detail and sell benefits. Show how solution will work to provide benefits to buying company and people, including them. Give examples. Stimulate prospect to imagine the solution being used in their environment. Discuss
Tries it	Tries out, usually on a demonstration or pilot basis. Weighs evidence of trial	Supporter and instructor	Guide and support positive reactions. Handle objections. Provide an actual trial demonstration. Guide them through it. Provide feedback. Provide opportunities for talking to others who have benefited. Use reference sells by telephone or in person. Be around to handle any problems when the prospect is weighing the evidence.

Levels of support	Signs	Your role	Possible actions
Committed	Accepts its worth and relevance, plans to use	Supporter	Support and maintain presence. Be around to prevent any event or person turning prospect against solution irrationally or inadvertently. Support use and deal with difficulties professionally. If possible manage the monitoring and evaluation. Reinforce and provide follow up support.
Internalizes	Becomes an enthusiastic user and supporter. Use of it becomes everyday behaviour. The win win is recognized	Ally	Capitalize on relationship of ally. Look for further opportunties and build on success. Capitalize on the change and possibly the relationships that have been made

○ *Add to your chart of the key people what you belive their current attitude to be.*

○ *Where you are unsure, plan how you are going to find out.*

FAST TRACK

You have now taken the first view of the personal position of the buyers and there is one other clue that you need.

are they driving or restraining and why?

Some people in the group will be driving the project positively. They may not yet be committed but they are pushing their colleagues to take the proposal seriously. Others will be restrainers. For some reason they hold back from supporting even the investigation of the relevance of the solution.

If we understand why people have adopted their stance as drivers or restrainers the team can plan what needs to be done to improve the position.

This list of possible sources of driving and restraining forces will be useful and prompt you to think of others. Remember that working on reducing restraining forces, on balance, will pay off more than increasing the driving forces.

- Cost.
- Attitude towards change.
- Alternative experience.
- Previous experience.
- Autonomy.
- Job security.
- Variety of work.
- Workload.
- Time.
- Management support.
- Reward system.
- Enthusiasm.
- Autonomy between divisions.

- Customary practices.
- Self development.
- Social contacts.
- Allegiance to other methods.
- Resources.
- Number or quality of allies.
- Skill or capability of self or others.
- Status or authority.
- Freedom.
- Organization.
- Policy.

FAST TRACK

○ *For each of the key people on your chart, add whether they are drivers or restrainers and the reason why.*

○ *Where you are unsure, plan how to find out.*

The account manager and the team has now completed the analysis part of the campaign plan. It is time to start planning the actual activities. A benefit of good planning is that if the team does the analysis phase well, the action plan and the milestones needed to achieve it will probably be fairly apparent.

> **Start planning the actual activities.**

From the analysis of the customer's business case we can see the gaps in our knowledge or in our gaining agreements from the key people.

Here are some examples of milestones which are concerned with the business issues:

- *By the end of next month, to have agreed the extent of the benefits case with the production manager.*

- *Before the major demonstration to have agreed the cost benefit analysis with the finance department.*

- *To be in a position to connect the proposal to at least one critical success factor which has been articulated by the decision- maker, before proposal time.*

Here are some milestones which are concerned with the people issues.

- *To have got the IT director to express some interest in the proposal, measured by her agreeing to attend a reference sell.*

- *To have agreed a joint plan with our champion to neutralize the antagonism of the IT department, before the managing director returns.*

- *To have agreed with the financial controller that a meeting with the finance director is in his interests as well.*

All of these objectives are driven by the environmental analysis. The essence of successful action plans is accountability and timescale.

The team then assigns the milestones to an individual member, who becomes responsible for that achievement in the timescale allowed. Members will have a lot of say on the timescale of their activities. After all they have to fit them into their schedules and give the team a strong sense that the actions involved will be done and the milestone achieved.

At this stage it can prove useful to use the action plan form from the campaign planning documentation (see Chapter 4).

9

account planning for working partnerships - 1

producing a plan to ensure the long-term relationship with the key account

---

The "bible" of the account manager is the key account plan. It includes a comprehensive statement of the situation in the two companies, sets out the short and long-term goals and finishes with an action plan which is the ultimate aim of planning.

the key account planning process

This chapter describes how a planning team goes about a key account planning session. The introduction covers the following points:

- Objectives of a key account planning session.
- Who is there.
- How long do you work.
- What do you need.

OBJECTIVES OF A KEY ACCOUNT PLANNING SESSION

A planning session starts from a vision or mission. We want to change, possibly dramatically, a part of the world to our vision of it. The mission could be very broad or very focused; but it gives the starting point of the plan.

The objective of a planning session is "To produce the best possible plan to achieve this mission". Notice how the objective breaks the rules of normal objectives - "best possible" is not an accurate measurement for achievement. We have to accept this though, as a more accurate test for success could constrain the creative thinking of the plan.

If for example the team set a mission "To capture 50% of the addressable market," it would have two problems. How does it know before the planning process that this is achievable, and how does it know that if it tried it could not achieve more?

EXAMPLE

Planning team mission statements

We wish to produce the best possible plan to achieve our mission:

- ○ To be the supplier of first choice to the account in all of Europe and North America.

- ○ To be and to be seen as a major supplier in the civil government market.

- ○ To improve our marketshare in the account worldwide. ▶

- To achieve at least 10 per cent higher level of revenue growth in the account every year for the next three years.

- To use our reputation in the pharmaceuticals division of the account to gain 10 per cent of the orders placed in the chemicals division within a year.

- *Define a mission statement for your chosen key account.*

FAST TRACK

WHO IS THERE   In Chapter 4 we looked at "The Pyramid of Plans" and the different planning teams which have to be formed for certain purposes. In this section we will limit ourselves to a key account team planning session. An example of the people involved is:

- **Account manager, account consultant, services consultant.**

- **Any other cross-functional account teams dedicated to parts of the account.**

- **An appropriate marketing person.**

- **Appropriate sub-accountees. We will use the term sub-accountee to describe an account manager or salesperson responsible for part of the account.**

It is likely that the team will comprise of between six and eight people. If it is the first time for the team the session will probably be at least three days.

If there is a facilitator, he or she will be responsible for describing and getting agreement to the ground rules of planning. He or she will also police and time the session to ensure that by the end the team has reached an appropriate point in the process.

Have a senior manager attend the last session of the key account planning event.

It is highly desirable to have a senior manager attend the last session of the key account planning event to hear a short presentation of the team's conclusions. This gives a focus to the team who will have to be ready to make such a presentation when the time comes.

FAST TRACK

○ *Choose whom you would invite to your planning session.*

HOW LONG DO YOU WORK?

Experience shows that after eight or nine hours the productivity of planners drops dramatically. It is probably better, therefore, to finish at around 17.30. If it is a new team or some new members are joining, it is a good idea to have the meeting off-site and to have dinner together. Don't forget, though, you are trying to make these planning events regular and routine. It is a good idea to call a one or two-day planning session to modify a particular part of the plan and to hold such a meeting in an ordinary conference room.

WHAT DO YOU NEED?

The only documentation you need will be incorporated on flipcharts by the end of the session. So, make sure you supply:

● **Two flipchart stands.**

● **Many pads of flipchart paper.**

● **Flipchart pens with at least the colours blue, red, green and black.**

● **Set the chairs, as comfortably as possible, in a semi-circle facing the flipcharts and the facilitator. Discourage tables and note pads.**

The key account plan outline

Fig 9.1

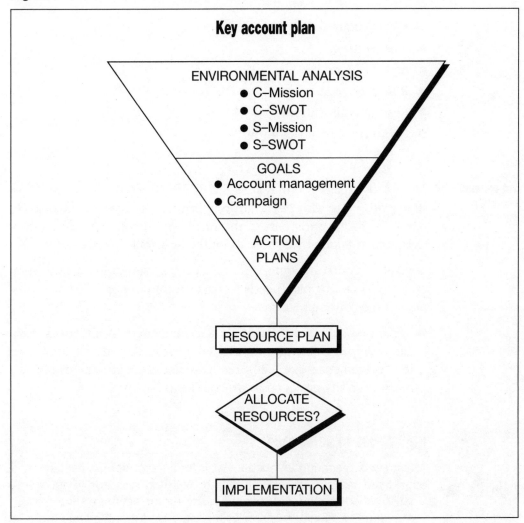

In trying to explain the upside down triangle we will start from an overview, and discuss each element in more detail later. The headings for the description are:

- The creative planning process.
- Database of knowledge.
- SWOT analysis.
- Goal setting.
- Activity planning.
- Resource plan.
- Resource allocation.
- Ground rules of planning.

THE CREATIVE
PLANNING
PROCESS

The word "creative" reminds us that we are looking for the best possible plan. Try to avoid all your prejudices and preconceived ideas. In particular in the early part of the planning process we will not constrain our thinking by doubts about the availability of resources.

We will of course recognize that there is a management budgeting cycle and that our plan needs to have resources approved at appropriate times during that cycle.

Nevertheless we need creative ideas to generate new initiatives. After all, any company's management can put resource where it likes. If we give management a good business case and enough time to react, it can resource any project that we could exploit.

EXAMPLE

High hopes in aerospace

A team was preparing an account plan for an aircraft manufacturer. It considered the strong position it had built and was agonizing over what the short to medium-term aspiration for marketshare should be.

At one point a junior member of the team said that the logic of the plan so far led to the fact that the account team's goal should be for 100 per cent of all large computers supplied.

At first rejected by the team as unrealistic, the members were slowly won over until that goal was set. They achieved customer Board approval of this some nine months later. The single vendor policy lasted two years during which the account team's order book swelled.

The team learnt good lessons from this, particularly that anyone in the team can make significant contributions through new insights. ○

Remember the Chinese proverb - do not decide where you want to go and how to get there until you are quite certain where you are now.

The team needs to understand the customer's business, the customer's industry, the customer's current financial and competitive environment, the influences of the general economy, etc.

That's before the team adds the supplier company environment, its current market strategies, position in the account, products and services, etc. If we have organized a huge database of knowledge, planning will become more and more effective.

For the moment let us imagine that either before, or during, the event the account manager has briefed the planning team on the information necessary to take part in the creation of the plan. It is useful to distinguish in the database between hard data and soft data.

> **Distinguish in the database between hard data and soft data.**

Hard data is defined as known facts which are normally historical. What were the customer's key ratios last year? How did they compare with the competition? How many employees does it have and how are they organized? That list has not even scratched the surface.

The team will never have all the facts at its fingertips. Indeed in a new account penetration plan there will be little information to hand and the planning session will be quite short, but the more information available to the team the better.

Soft data is in many ways as important or even more important than hard data. It includes all the prejudices and politics of the people side of the business. This data consists of the subjective opinions drawn by customer managers or the account team.

WATCH OUT!

Do not take things at face value

In any large company there is an organization chart. It is hard data. It says: "That person reports to that person, who reports to that person, who reports to that person, etc".

The soft data asks: "Yes, but who actually runs the business, who has influence, who can make things happen and equally – who can stop things happening?"

In many large British companies there is a network of people with similar backgrounds who, though in different divisions and at different levels in the business, form a powerful *virtual team*.

In one very large privatized business the organization chart did not reveal - without further examination - the fact that many established and up and coming executives had not only attended the same university, but also the same college.

The environment section of a creative planning process includes the background knowledge including the soft data brought by everyone in the team.

SWOT ANALYSIS

The analysis technique which we use for sorting out our knowledge and different team members' angles on the plan is called SWOT analysis - **Strengths, Weaknesses, Opportunities and Threats**.

This is a simple technique, as so many good ones are, for helping the team to understand what it needs to do in the account.

Unfortunately, like all techniques it can be implemented well and therefore also badly. Further guidance on good SWOT analysis follows, so suffice it to say at this point that a comprehensive, well-documented SWOT analysis makes the next part of the planning process reasonably straightforward.

> **It can be implemented well and therefore also badly.**

The objective of SWOT analysis is not simply to describe the environment, rather it is to describe the environment in a way which helps us to understand what we need to do.

It is in two parts, the customer SWOT (C-SWOT) and the supplier SWOT (S-SWOT).

Once we have got an agreed description of the environment we can decide what to do about it.

GOAL SETTING   Following the use of a bridging technique which ensures that the work done in the SWOT analysis is fully exploited, the team sets its goals. In a key account plan goals are divided into account management goals and campaign goals.

Account management goals are the relationship goals and tend to be more strategic and longer term than campaign goals. Experience has enabled us to break down account management goals into eight goal areas.

Not all plans will require goals in all eight areas but all plans will require goals in some of these areas. The detail of this follows, but for the sake of example, three of these goal areas are:

- **Level of contact.**

- **Customer satisfaction.**

- **Marketshare.**

Campaign goals are goals where a major milestone is taking an order from a customer for the supplier's products and/or services. It is likely that campaign goals will be "owned" by a sub-accountee or the salesperson responsible for the campaign rather than the account manager. The methods used for campaign planning are explained in Chapters 5-8.

Having decided what we want to achieve, we come to the last part of the planning process - the activity plans.

ACTIVITY PLANNING   It is very much a personal decision as to the amount of detail into which activity plans have to go. Some people are comfortable with macro actions and milestones which are weeks or even months apart. Other people try to plan all the activities required to achieve the goal in the minutest detail, even down to a telephone call.

It is personal preference. Either will do as long as it achieves the aim of activity planning which is to estimate the resources required to achieve the goal.

The team should now be in a position to produce its best forecast of its achievements in the account both short-term and long-term and the amount of resource investment required from the supplying company to achieve these results.

The resource plan is actually a re-sort of the activity plan. If we know what has to be done and who has to do it we can produce our best estimate of the resources required.

This enables us to move to the next step in the planning process. This is either part of the normal budgeting cycle or on some occasions a special case to take to management as a long or short-term business investment plan.

It is vital to narrow down an accurate definition of the resources which will implement the plan. Too often the team starts to implement the early part of the plan, only to find a resource problem later.

> **Narrow down an accurate definition of the resources which will implement the plan.**

The team needs to get itself into good order to move to the next step which is to persuade management to put those resources at the team's disposal.

Most account plans require resources which are not in the direct control of the account team. A decision box occurs therefore when management decides on the merits of the various plans being put forward and allocates its resources. We should try to see this as a contract.

The account team is saying to the appropriate level of management "I will give you these results", meaning the goals, "if you will give me these resources". If management says yes, either immediately or as the budgeting cycle grinds on, the team implements the plan.

If management says no, the team adjusts its goals and resubmits, because, of course, no planning process is complete until the resources have been allocated to its implementation.

Be careful. Management can often from its wider experience offer short cuts towards account teams' goals and therefore legitimately reduce the amount of resource required to achieve the result.

However, in an immature planning cycle, management, particularly sales management, has a habit of liking the sound of the result, but not allocating the resource in full.

At worst this leads to teams second guessing the likelihood of their getting resources when they are setting goals and completely constrains the creativity of the plan.

For their part, account teams must recognize that while management can get any resource required to achieve a well constructed business plan, it requires more than a week's notice. The plans must signal in detail this year's resource requirement and broadly the requirement of the subsequent two years, particularly if special or unusual resources are going to be required.

In this opening we have looked in outline at the key account planning process. More detail on each element follows a statement on the disciplines required from the planning team during the process.

GROUND RULES OF PLANNING The ground rules are concerned with the efficiency of the planning session. Where two or three people are gathered together you will find differences of opinion, multiple ideas, different angles on the same topic, personal prejudices and all the other features of a team of human beings.

These tend to reduce the efficiency of a team. It is the job of the facilitator and of course of the team itself, to maintain a number of disciplines.

1. Talk and document in short, simple but complete sentences

This item is proved in the detail on SWOT analysis, and is probably the most important rule. If we talk in bullet points then we will get quick agreement to a rough definition of the key issues. However, what we need is the agreement of the team to a detailed statement of the *real meaning* of the key issue.

2. Equal voice/Equal vote

In a creative planning session, rank disappears. It is vital that the planning team does not believe that it is there to wait until the senior person has expressed a view and then agree with it.

Real creativity may easily come from a member of the team who is the most junior and therefore the least experienced. So, account managers, a sure way to kill the creativity of your team is to make it plain, after about an hour of planning, that the only plan which is going to be acceptable is the one you had in your head before the meeting started.

Remember that to get a team committed to a plan of action you must encourage it to take part in the planning process. Avoid telling them what they are going to do, like a prophet with tablets of stone. In the end, however, the team has to get to a plan.

The difference between equal voice and equal vote is best shown by an example. In a discussion about where to go on holiday, children have an equal voice, they can say where they want to go, but they certainly don't have a vote.

The account manager's neck is on the block, so in extreme cases he or she may have to use some assertiveness to get to a satisfactory conclusion.

In practice there are rarely problems in this area. The team is pleased to be part of the planning process and will normally get amicably to the necessary consensus.

3. 100 per cent agreement

Allied to the above is the rule of 100 per cent agreement. Read literally this means that no part of the plan is firm until all members of the team have agreed with it.

It is important. Most planning sessions produce new directions and new activities for all of the members of the team. In

Most planning sessions produce new directions.

many cases these will be in addition to or different from the activities which the team member has underway.

If the momentum of the plan is to be kept up and the new directions implemented, it is vital that everyone agrees and that the timescales and resources have been accurately forecast.

If this rule goes wrong you will find that people are not disagreeing with a part of the plan simply because they have in fact no intention of carrying out their role in it. "They can write it up if they want, it ain't going to happen."

4. Do not duck issues

Following on the 100 per cent agreement, a successful planning session tables and discusses all the key issues surrounding the plan. Here are some examples of issues which are frequently ducked.

- A person agrees to an activity, but team members do not believe he or she has the necessary knowledge or skills to carry it out.

- A necessary activity is in someone else's province and we duck the issue of how to get that person's buy into the plan.

- An activity is agreed which has a dependency on higher management agreement and no plan is put in place to gain this.

- An activity is agreed which has a dependency on the customer's part and no plan is put in place to ensure that the customer can and does achieve the dependency.

5. Think before you speak

We will not keep to this rigidly because sometimes people do think through an idea while they are articulating it. However, it is a useful rule to agree before the planning session starts so that we can use it to muffle someone who frequently waffles.

The facilitator will present these rules to the team and given that they agree to abide by them, the planning session proper can begin.

FAST TRACK

○ *Decide who should be your facilitator – a person outside the planning team.*

○ *Agree the process with the facilitator.*

10

account planning for working partnerships - 2

completing the environmental analysis stage of the key account planning process

---

Defining the scope of the planning session and evaluating the customer's current situation. Testing the strengths and weaknesses of the selling team's situation and defining a set of account management criteria.

step by step through the environmental analysis

- STEP 1 – Agree the Customer-Mission.

- STEP 2 – The Customer-SWOT.

- STEP 3 – Agree the Supplier-Mission.

- STEP 4 – The Supplier-SWOT.

- STEP 5 – Cross check the Customer-SWOT to the Supplier-SWOT.

STEP 1   Agree the Customer-Mission

Normally the driving force of an account team's plan will be a statement of a customer aim – in the planning process. This is the customer mission statement or C-Mission. This can be huge or small, a corporate aim or a focused project.

Be careful not to bite off more than the team can chew. It is better to do a high quality plan on a single division, rather than a less well informed plan on the whole organization.

Take a company like the Pearson Group which is a group incorporating many companies. Its strategy is to divide the group into three global markets aimed at information, education and entertainment.

An account team which has a strong presence in say the publishing part of Pearson might very well limit the account plan to the information companies. Still plenty of scope, but focused on that part of the business the team knows best.

If the team is experienced and has strength in all parts of the account it is planning, then it will start with the vision of the company in question.

Vision statements tend to follow a pattern. They start from an aspiration to a continuing achievement "To be...". This is followed by a superlative for example "the best" or "the most successful". There follows a description of the business or business operation and a geographic area.

A major American bank has the vision statement: "To be the best financial services provider in the world".

A UK police force: "To be the envy of every other force in the country".

The Automobile Association (AA) in the UK: "To be the UK's leading and most successful personal assistance organization." ○

If the planning team chooses such a broad mission as the driver of the planning session, it will take a very comprehensive view of the account.

Here are some examples of mission statements which are more limited in their scope.

C-Mission for a telecommunications company: "To reduce our dependency on BT by achieving one sale to Mercury by end December 1990".

A food manufacturer: "To continue our rapid growth of business in Russia". ○

In both cases these are pretty focused C-Missions leading to activities which are channelled into one particular issue in the account.

It is important to get the C-Mission right as it kicks off the direction and scope of the planning session. But the team must not become inflexible. If during the next stage of the process it finds the mission statement to be slightly or wholly wrong, it does not normally take much effort to change it and correct all the subsequent work.

It is likely that the account manager will have the C-Mission prepared before the start of the planning session. Once the whole team has agreed the message and content of the C-Mission it is stuck on the wall in a prominent position and remains,

Have the C-Mission prepared before the start of the planning session.

throughout the session, a helpful reminder of the scope of the session.

You will find it very useful from time to time to check in other parts of the session that the team is still limiting the scope of its discussion to the C-Mission.

○ *Make an attempt to define the C-Mission for your plan.*

The C-SWOT

I like to use a pretty broad definition of the terms strengths, weaknesses, opportunities and threats. It is more important that all the key issues are identified and documented than that the team sticks rigidly to a narrow definition of the sections. Working definitions if the team needs them are:

- **Strengths** are facts or events which will assist the customer in achieving the mission.

- **Weaknesses** are facts or events which will hinder the customer from achieving the mission.

- **Opportunities** are things that the customer could do which will improve the chances of achieving the mission.

- **Threats** are facts or events which, if not addressed, will prevent the customer from achieving the mission.

Onto a flip chart write the following: "In terms of achieving that mission the customer has the following:

STRENGTHS   Under this heading, in short, simple but complete sentences outline the strengths which the customer could exploit in striving to achieve the mission.

C-strengths

- The customer has the technical resources and skills.

- The necessary investment money is available.

- Top management is committed to the mission.

- They can leverage from the reputation gained in their large installed base.

- The company is represented in all the parts of the world on which it wishes to focus.

Some teams like to start from a series of bullet points and then expand them into sentences. As we will see, however, it is much easier to proceed to the next part of the process if the team eventually obeys the discipline of short, simple but complete sentences.

It is very useful to distinguish the SWOT analysis by colour. Use blue for strengths, red for weaknesses, green for opportunities and black for threats. As the team completes each chart, pin or stick it to the wall. It is then a relatively simple task to locate SWOT statements later in the process.

WEAKNESSES

Under this heading, in short, simple but complete sentences outline the weaknesses which the customer will have to acknowledge in his plan or correct in his plan in striving to achieve the mission.

C-weaknesses

● **Some ageing plant cannot achieve the required productivity.**

● **Some managers will not agree to the necessary changes to their jobs if the mission is to be achieved.**

● **Some managers cannot learn the new skills which are necessary.**

● **We cannot expand department X because there is no pool of skilled labour available.**

Spend enough time on the weaknesses section as it will probably contain the germs of the selling company's opportunities. Having said that, keep the SWOT broad and focused on the customer, not on the products and services which you sell.

The team is trying to ensure that the plan is driven by the customer and his requirements.

OPPORTUNITIES

We must be more flexible in the opportunities section on the sentences discipline. In this case, bullet points may suffice. What is needed here is a creative brainstorm of all the things the customer could do to try and reach the C-Mission.

Let it all hang out and do not reject anything at this stage. We will have an opportunity subsequently to check the feasibility of the ideas with the customer.

C-opportunities

- Gather marketing information on pricing, potential customers and competition.

- Change the career paths for key middle managers.

- Invest in communications technology.

- Sell the chemicals division.

- Re-engineer all the current business processes.

- Delegate industrial relations policy to the business units.

At this point the team must make an important check to ensure that there is consistency between the weaknesses and opportunities part of the SWOT analysis.

Before moving on to the threats part of the analysis process, get the team to check through the weaknesses section of the SWOT.

Has the team identified improvements or changes which the customer could make to address each and every one of the weaknesses? This ensures the comprehensiveness of the opportunities section.

Address each and every one of the weaknesses.

THREATS

Threats have a dual function. On the one hand they describe potential disruptions to the customer mission from external and often uncontrollable sources.

External C-threats

- If top management does not settle the working practices and demarcation problems we cannot achieve the productivity required to meet the mission.

- If the price of oil rises above $40 per barrel the profitability aim is not achievable.

- If the government privatizes electricity generation our current sales structure will become ineffective.

On the other hand, it is often useful in the threats column to document what will happen if the weaknesses identified above are not addressed or if the mission statement is not achieved.

Internal C-threats

- If we fail to achieve the productivity aims in the mission statement, top management will invest elsewhere.

- The competition could catch up with our product advantage.

The C-SWOT stretches the account team's customer knowledge to its limits and frequently produces a "We do not know" list which fits into the supplier weaknesses part of the SWOT analysis.

The stronger the C-SWOT the more customer oriented is the resulting plan.

Of course the ultimate in C-SWOT is to persuade the customer to go through the process with the supplier account team. This joint planning is an aiming point for most account teams and we will look at it again in the section on organization.

In any case the account manager should take the C-SWOT to the customer. Most executives are very impressed by the fact that the selling team has gone to such lengths in trying to provide solutions. Psychologically they are in a position where they will probably want to agree with some of the statements and correct or modify others.

Number each of the Strengths, Weaknesses, Opportunities and Threats individually when it is agreed that the C-SWOT has been completed.

This number is simply for reference purposes so that we can refer to, for example, weakness 15 and the team can quickly locate it in the red section of the SWOT analysis.

○ *Write some examples of C-SWOT statements for your key account.*

FAST TRACK

STEP 3   ## Agree the Supplier-Mission

The S-Mission is an outline aim of what the supplier wants to achieve in the part of the customer's business described in the C-Mission and C-SWOT.

We discussed it in the objective part of the previous chapter.

S-Mission statements

EXAMPLE

"To be acknowledged as the natural choice for our type of products and services."

EXAMPLE

"To improve our market share in chemicals division."

EXAMPLE

"To break into the commercial department for the first time by proving that investment in our products and services will assist the department in its productivity targets."

EXAMPLE

"To optimize our sales during this company year."

EXAMPLE

"To be the leading supplier in the account."

As with the C-Mission, the S-Mission can be very broad or more focused. If, however, the focus is more or less on one sales objective the team should check whether key account planning is the appropriate

Be flexible and find the way which suits your team.

process, or whether it would be better off doing a campaign plan.

It is likely that the account manager will bring the S-Mission with him or her, in which case it only requires the team to buy into it before the supplier part of the environmental analysis starts in earnest.

If it is helpful, many teams start the whole planning session with the S-Mission. They find that they need that focus before starting on the customer analysis. Be flexible and find the way which suits your team.

STEP 4   The S-SWOT

Onto a flip chart write: "In terms of achieving that mission we have the following:"

STRENGTHS

Under this heading, in short, simple but complete sentences outline the strengths which your company could exploit in striving to achieve the S-Mission.

An example of a badly stated strength is the bullet point "installed base". Ask yourselves the "so what?" question. We have a large installed base but so what? Better would be "Our installed base means that we have good technical and financial references in chemicals division".

Use the "so what" question wherever the team is having trouble agreeing on a particular element of the SWOT.

S-strengths

● If we have good reason it is simple for us to gain access to senior management and keep our information up to date.

● Our position as market leader means that we already have the necessary credibility to provide major solutions.

● We can mirror the global organization of the customer.

● The company is prepared to work with small and therefore flexible suppliers.

WEAKNESSES   Under this heading, in short, simple but complete sentences outline the weaknesses which you will have to acknowledge or correct in the plan in striving to achieve the S-Mission.

A poor weakness statement would be "IBM domination". This begs the question and does not help us to know what to do. Better would be "IBM has more control over the customer's IT strategy than we do". In this latter case the statement helps us to see what to do next.

S-weaknesses

● We have less senior management contact than our principal competitor.

● The current product is not as useable as the one planned for launch in three months.

● The north-west region has had an interrupted delivery pattern.

● Our senior management has not agreed that the customer should be a special case for early product launch.

OPPORTUNITIES   We must be more flexible in the opportunities section on the sentences discipline. In this case, bullet points may suffice. What is needed here is a creative brainstorm of all the things the team and the supplying company could do to try and reach the S-Mission.

Maximize your creativity, because this is where we employ the vision to change the world in your company's direction.

S-opportunities

● Organize a joint planning session.

● Run a series of road shows to enable the director of telecommunications to keep the people in the divisions up to date.

● Sell a consultancy project to report on the feasibility of a Call Centre approach.

THREATS   Threats have a dual function. On the one hand they describe potential disruptions to the S-Mission from external and often uncontrollable sources.

On the other hand, it is often useful in the threats column to document what will happen if the weaknesses identified above are not addressed or if the mission statement is not achieved.

Just as in the weaknesses, it is poor practice to put the name of a major competitor as a threat. After all, if the threat is simply the name of a company, all you could do to remove the threat is buy them, shoot them or join them.

Better would be "If we fail to have more influence over the customer's IT strategy, a major competitor will be the decision-maker when we are asked to bid".

Notice how the SWOT analysis describes the environment, it does not decide what we are going to do. For example, that last threat could be a perfectly sensible way of running that part of the account in a highly productive way. It basically means if we are asked to bid we will win. We may decide therefore to deploy our resources elsewhere and live with that threat.

S-threats

- The customer Board could decide it is too dependent on our products and services and encourage competition to win some market share.

- The part of the business where we are strong could be sold.

- All the work we are doing at technical level could be invalidated by a Board decision to invest elewhere.

The S-SWOT and its quality are the key to the success of the plan.

The S-SWOT and its quality are the key to the success of the plan.

○ *Write some examples of your S-SWOT statements.*

Cross-check the C-SWOT to the S-SWOT

You will notice that in composing the S-SWOT, the team makes frequent reference to the C-SWOT. At this point there is a specific check which is worth doing.

The weaknesses section of the C-SWOT describes the key issues which the customer has to do something about to achieve his aim. We must ensure that there is a corresponding supplier opportunity for as many of these weaknesses as possible.

Often they will not be technology opportunities or anything to do with our normal products and services. They may, for example, be opportunities to help the customer plan or review some business process or policy.

As a good example I have seen a plan for supplier personnel people to meet with the customer's personnel department to discuss mutually interesting topics. There is an infinite variety of possibilities.

If there is no connection between the customer's weaknesses and the supplier's opportunities, we have a major problem since we are not assisting the customer either through technology or otherwise to address his key issues.

That check being complete, we only need the S-SWOT as the reference point for goal setting. The C-SWOT can be ignored as all the key customer issues have come through to the plan via the S-opportunities.

EXAMPLE

Getting at the real problems of health care

An account team was selling to the UK national health service. At the time the NHS was going through enormous change in its management organization and method of working.

The NHS was implementing a fund-holding system which altered financial responsibility and gave new power to the administrative managers as opposed to the health professionals. The process had been going on for some time, and looked as though change would remain a major issue for many years.

When the selling team did the customer SWOT, the list of weaknesses was very long and included many management problems. In many cases there were problems getting staff agreement to the changes. Training was lagging behind the need for different *modus operandi* and staff morale was falling, in some cases dramatically. All this was feeding through to the quality of patient care. ▶

EXAMPLE

The team who knew the account well made a good job of documenting these weaknesses. When it came to carry out the supplier opportunities section, however, they concentrated on those areas of opportunity where it could sell their normal products and services.

On doing the C-SWOT to S-SWOT check, the team found that very few of its opportunities were hitting the key management issues of the account.

This was a very useful check and the team started to think much more broadly about how its experience in, for example, change management could be brought to bear to help the NHS with the real problems. An imaginative and profitable plan emerged and the role of a supplier in a working partnership was effectively demonstrated. ○

what next?

All round the room is a logical progression from the C-Mission through the C-SWOT, S-Mission and S-SWOT on flipcharts. We now need to decide what to do and we need to control the connection between the SWOT analysis and our activities.

○ *Do the C-SWOT to S-SWOT cross check for the examples you have produced.*

FAST TRACK

11

account planning for working partnerships – 3

assessing the selling team's position

By performing a "health check" on the selling team's situation in the account, we can start to see the overall position and then devise a plan to improve and exploit that. The team needs to agree on the critical success factors of account management in their business. How do you define a satisfactory working relationship?

step by step through the team assessment process

The team now needs a bridging mechanism which will act as a connector between the SWOT analysis and goal-setting. Without this simple device it is very difficult to get a good link and to know where to start.

A bit like eating an elephant (start by eating the tail) this bridge and the spider's web technique helps the team to move efficiently into the next phase of the plan.

There are three steps in this:

- STEP 1 – Agree the account team's critical success factors.

- STEP 2 – Produce the control matrix.

- STEP 3 – Agree the spider's web.

| STEP 1 | **Agree the account team's critical success factors** |

Experience has helped to define some general critical success factors (CSF) for professional account management. Starting from these, the team should decide which of them is 100 per cent relevant to its situation, which need modification and which, if any, need to be scrapped or replaced by another.

The detail of these goals will be discussed at Step 3, but you need a working definition at this stage.

In any key account there are some policy or strategy statements which have a major impact on the selling team's ability to do business.

Account management	Short definition
Level of contact	Assesses how well the team is placed to get to all the key people in the account
Customer satisfaction/supplier contribution	Measures how well we have kept our promises and provided customer satisfaction. Also measures whether or not the selling team has agreed with the customer the contribution it and its products and services have made to the customer's business
Account planning	Looks at the state and quality of the team's plans - both account plans and campaign plans
Competitive position	Looks at the two issues of protecting current market share and increasing it
Strategic applications, products and services	Assesses the fit between the customer's way ahead and the products and services of the supplying company in terms of strategic importance and leverage
Key customer strategies	In any key account there are some policy or strategy statements which have a major impact on the selling team's ability to do business. The team agrees at this stage how positive or negative these strategies are for its continuing success
Pipeline	Measures the team's sales pipeline to ensure that there are enough opportunities for making sales in the short to medium term to achieve its business targets
Market share	Looks at the overall trend of market share

Before moving on to the next step the team should revise its S-SWOT in the light of the account management critical success factors. Here is a checklist of questions in each of the areas:

Account management CSF	Checklist of sub-questions
Level of contact	• Do you have regular contacts at all levels? • Senior management? • High level within the product users? • High and wide at technical level? • Where necessary in central purchasing?
Customer satisfaction/ supplier contribution	• Do you have an agreed measure of customer satisfaction with the customer? • Do you deliver what you promised on time and within budget? • Does the product give the expected performance? • Is there a method of calculating the return on investment of previous projects you have supplied?
Account planning	• Does the account plan have the agreement of all the team members worldwide? • Does the pyramid of plans which links the main account plan to sub-account plans exist? • Do you have campaign plans in place for all major sales campaigns? • Have all the necessary resources agreed to make their contribution to all your plans?
Competitive position	• Are you aware of the strengths and weaknesses of the main competitors you are facing? • Are you aware of your company's strengths and weaknesses in relation to the competition? • How vulnerable is your installed base to competitive attack? • Are you seen as price competitive and value for money?

Account management CSF	Checklist of sub-questions
Strategic applications, products and services	• Has previous work which you have done got you into a position where what you supply is strategically important to the customer? • Can you leverage other sales from previous ones? • Do you currently have a proposal to make which will have this strategic impact?
Key customer strategies	• Is the team thoroughly aware of your company's product strategy and can it articulate it to your customer? • Is there a good connection between your plan and your customer's overall strategy? • Can you see the connection between your plan and some customer critical success factors?
Pipeline	• Do you know early enough in the customer's buying process when bids are being invited? • Do you have enough prospects in the pipeline to ensure that you will make target even if your biggest project fails to close? • Have you got a plan for regular prospecting for new opportunities?
Market share	• Do you have an acceptable measure of what your market share is? • Do your campaigns deliver market share in line with your company's goals?

○ *Review and amend the account management goal areas to meet your requirement.*

FAST TRACK

Produce the control matrix

The situation now is that the team has generated a SWOT analysis which encompasses all the key issues of its environment. It will be quite long. Maybe 15 Strengths, 30 Weaknesses, 15 Opportunities and 5 Threats.

Before turning to goal setting, the team needs to group the SWOT analysis into manageable parts. We need to allocate each Strength, Weakness, Opportunity and Threat to an account management goal area.

The method is this:

1. Number the SWOT analysis so that each Strength, Weakness, Opportunity and Threat is identifiable.

2. Now draw the control matrix as on the following chart.

3. Being careful to obey the colour code. Ask the team to group the SWOT analysis. In about three-quarters of an hour the team will identify each Weakness, Opportunity and Threat with one goal area.

Obey this rule if possible – *Only allocate a Weakness, Opportunity or Threat to one goal area*. As we will see at goal setting and action planning, we are getting near allocating responsibility for the achievement of progress in the plan to individuals. Each W, O and T will probably represent a milestone in the activity plan. It is important therefore that no action falls between two people's responsibility. Thus the rule.

> **Only allocate a Weakness, Opportunity or Threat to one goal area.**

When it comes to Strengths, we may of course put each Strength into as many goal areas as possible. At action planning time, the team will use the Strengths as pointers to what they can exploit to eliminate Weaknesses.

Agree the Spider's Web

The team is now in position, before moving to goal setting, to use the spider's web technique to assess our overall position in the account. The spider's web derives from the agreed critical success factors of good account management.

Control matrix chart

Goal area	Remove weakness	Exploit opportunity	Avoid threat	Use strength
Level of contact	1,,8,9,17,23	3,4,8,9,14	1,3,4	1,3,4,6,8,12
Customer satisfaction/ supplier contribution	2,3,7,15,16	1,2,5	2,6,10	2,4,6,8,10,
Account planning	20,21,22	6,10,11,12	7,8,11	1,3,4,7,8,9
Competitive position	4,5,6,10,11, 12	7,13	5,9	2,8,9,12
Strategic applications, products and services	1,17,24	16		2,7,8,9,11
Key customer strategies	13,14,18,19, 20	15	12,13	13,14
Pipeline	25,27	19,22	14,15	9,11,13
Market share	26,28,29	17,18,20,21	16	2,8,12,13

The assessment consists of the team marking itself subjectively out of 10 in each of the eight areas. 0 out of 10 - very bad position, 10 out of 10 - could not be better. In the example below it is assumed that the team is looking at the key account as a whole and that the selling company is a systems integrator selling a whole variety of hardware, software and consultancy products.

It is of course possible, and desirable, to make the assessment at many if not all levels inside a large account. In this case each sub-accountee will maintain this diagrammatic representation of the health of his or her part of the account.

LEVEL OF CONTACT 10/10 would mean that the supplier has regular business meetings at top level and very widely in the account. The test is height and width. A good score would reflect talking at top level, at high level within the user community and at top level in the IT organization.

A poor performance would reflect, for example, the only contact being in the IT department of a subsidiary where the supplier has done business.

Notice the contact must be at business meetings. If we only meet the chief executive once a year at the ballet, that fails the test of top level contact.

This is a very key test because if the team scores low here then other goal areas are made impossible to do well, eg account planning.

CUSTOMER SATISFACTION/ SUPPLIER CONTRIBUTION As with many of these goal areas this test breaks into 2 marks out of 5 rather than 1 out of 10.

Customer satisfaction This reflects the normal supplier measure of customer satisfaction. Did we deliver what we promised on time and within budget? Does the hardware and software give the expected up-time? When there are problems, are they fixed quickly? Are we supporting the sites properly?

A customer satisfaction survey gives good clues for this test; but it should be remembered that such a survey reflects what the customer believes is good customer satisfaction.

What we really need here is a test of what the customer believes and agrees with us is a satisfactory performance.

Top rate account managers will negotiate with the customer a level of satisfaction which the customer finds acceptable and which the account manager can sell internally to those parts of the supplier organization which are involved in delivering the promises.

Supplier contribution This measures the agreed impact that projects previously implemented by the supplier have had on the customer's business. The keys are reductions in costs, avoidance of costs, improved decision-making and control. In other words, return on investment (RoI).

We will score highly here if we are involved in the cost/benefit analysis which the customer does before investing and also involved in measuring the impact of projects once implemented – the audit function.

Score low if we are unaware of the processes the customer has in place for estimating RoI or if the customer never does any post-hoc cost justification.

This is an area where teams can achieve competitive edge if it is the only supplier who tries to help the customer to do this. There is no better opening to a presentation of a new project than to open with the positive business impact of previous projects.

> **Score low if we are unaware of the processes the customer has.**

ACCOUNT PLANNING

What is the state of our account planning? Do we have a plan which meets the rules of a top quality plan? A top quality plan:

- Is approved by everyone involved.
- Reflects customer's own business plan.
- Has predicted results which are stretching but credible.
- Includes identified and committed resources from the supplier and the customer.
- Is backed by a huge "knowledge database" of customer's environment.
- Conforms to a standard format where one is in place.
- Includes clearly identified key dependencies.
- Contains measurable milestones for all objectives.
- Is regularly updated to reflect change and team achievements.
- Incorporates ideas derived "top down" and "bottom up".
- Stands alone as a communication of an account team's intentions.

A high score here will mean that the customer has been involved at some point in the planning process and that those parts of the plan which he needs to agree are complete and agreed.

Notice that it is impossible for the plan to reflect the customer's own business plan if the team scores poorly on level of contact.

The team also scores itself for the state of its campaign plans for crucial sales situations.

COMPETITIVE POSITION

This breaks into two parts.

a) How vulnerable is our installed base? Is any of it under competitive attack? Would it be relatively easy for the customer to remove our presence and replace our products and services with competitive ones?

b) Looking into the future, do our strengths against the competition give us a fighting chance of breaking into competitive areas? The key here is to understand what the strengths and weaknesses are of our product portfolio and the competition's.

STRATEGIC APPLICATIONS, PRODUCTS AND SERVICES

This looks at the leverage which can come from the installed base or from an identified potential sale. Has what we have already sold given us significant competitive edge for future projects and made a strategic contribution to the customer's business?

Score highly if so and also highly if such a strategic application, product or service is being actively considered by the customer for future implementation.

If such a project is being considered we may need a heavier weight of resources in relation to the supplier short-term benefit.

KEY CUSTOMER STRATEGIES

A two-part question:

a) Does the customer strategy broadly reflect the supplier's approach? Is it easy to see a link between the supplier's product and services strategy and the main customer policies which have a major impact on our ability to make sales?

The team must first reach a decision as to which customer strategies are involved. In the computer industry, the key strategy will be the one (or ones) which concern IT and telecommunications.

Keep your thinking wide. This is not just a question of, for example a technology strategy, it is also concerned with the customer's strategic requirements, management strategy and business processes.

b) Are we, the supplying team involved in the process which the customer uses to review these strategies? A systems integrator scores highly here if it is continuously asked for opinions and for input to strategic IT planning. The same team scores low if that position is held by a competitor.

PIPELINE

In order to improve market share we need to have identified where and when the customer is going to invest. This investment programme shows the rate of growth of the market and allows us to forecast what our short and medium-term revenues are going to be.

A full pipeline of potential business which covers what we need to sell in order to meet our market share aspiration many times over gives a high score here.

A high score should also mean that the team is less vulnerable to a delay in one large project by the customer throwing the whole plan into disarray.

We also need to know early in the customer's buying process when bids are being invited. A good score in this reflects the fact that the systems integrator is involved heavily in the applications strategy.

The supplier is probably also helping the customer in project evaluation before the customer gets to the nitty gritty of choosing hardware and software. A poor score could be caused by the fact that we only know about a bid when the specification lands on our desk, or where the customer makes a lot of hardware and software investments without our participation or even knowledge.

MARKET SHARE

In the end, this is what it is all about.

Using a sensible measure, is our market share significant, and is it rising? The litmus test of successful account management is whether over a long period of time we win against the competition.

> **We can now get a pictorial image by drawing the spider's web.**

Taking these critical success factors we can now get a pictorial image by drawing the spider's web. Here is an example from a Universal Systems' customer:

Fig 11.1

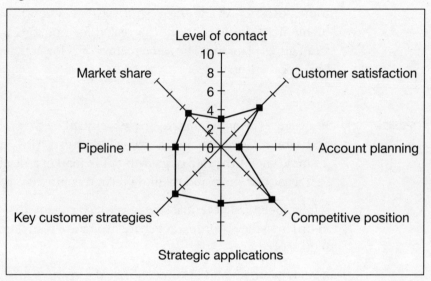

Universal Systems Integration has sold technical computers into a number of divisions of a large corporation. However, one large division is a recent acquisition to the group and is a heavy Universal user for commercial and technical applications.

We recently bid for and won a contract to supply the hardware and software for the building of a communications network. The spider's web is explained like this:

Level of contact (score 3)

We have never spoken to top management at corporate level. In the division where we are strong we have slumped to an IT-only contact, with the division's general manager meeting us socially from time to time.

Customer satisfaction/Universal contribution (score 6)

We have performed well and score highly on the customer satisfaction survey. However, we do not know if the customer measures RoI before or after investment We are not sure either what the network is supposed to achieve for the business, beyond - "we need to be able to talk to each other".

Account planning (score 2)

We have hardly started this and are blocked from getting the process going by our poor level of contact.

Competitive position (score 8)

It would take a very long time indeed to get rid of the Universal installed base. Our position as the network supplier will tend to give us early warning of future bids.

Strategic Applications, Products and Services (Score 6)

The leverage from the network is crucial for us, the network crucial for the customer. We do not really know how to exploit this.

Key customer strategies (score 7)

The network oriented approach should prove suitable for the customer's business strategy of export-led market growth. There is an agreed and recent IT strategy at Board level; but it is not well sold to the divisions. Its decentralized tone should suit us; but we are not really involved in discussing the long term.

The customer has a problem with the role of its long established central IT department. Its rather autocratic approach could conflict with the new strategy for IT. They still tend to believe that a user initiative out in the divisions to make investment is a failure on central IT's part and an extravagance on the user's. If the role continues as it is we will continue to be kept at arm's length from senior managers and users.

Pipeline (score 5)

Our pipeline is not sufficient to reflect our new market share. We do not understand the opportunities at corporate or divisional level outside our own strong division

Market share (score 5)

Our market share has just increased significantly and will continue to do so in the short term as the network is implemented. The key to maintaining that momentum is to discover more opportunities in the pipeline.

○ *From your knowledge of the account, make an assessment of your score in the goal areas and draw your spider's web.*

FAST TRACK

12

account planning for working partnerships - 4

setting objectives and planning activities

We now know the current position in the account and have a good analysis of our strengths and weaknesses. It is time to prioritize these and as a team set our aspirations for the account. We will use the power of well-composed team objectives to change the world.

setting the account management goals for the account

First of all a bit of revision on the attributes of a well-worded objective or goal. It must be:

- **Stretching.**

- **Measurable.**

- **Achievable.**

- **Related to the customer.**

- **Time targeted.**

We have seen the relatively concrete version of this in setting campaign goals. In that case there is a specific customer problem and a specific measurable solution for the team to propose.

Account management goals reflect the longer term relationship between the two companies.

Account management goals are more diffi-cult. They reflect the longer term relation-ship between the two companies and deal with the quality of that rela-tionship as well as with other measures which are easier to quantify.

The **SMART** template is more difficult to apply to account manage-ment goals. The team will have to allow more flexibility without compromising the aim of a goal which is to make it possible for the team to monitor its success in implementing the plan.

Taking the spider's web depicted at the end of the last chapter, the team is able to look first at the priority areas which are the points on which it scores lowest.

It makes sense therefore for the team in the previous chapter to spend the start of the goal setting session agreeing what to do in the areas of:

- Level of contact.

- Account planning.

- Pipeline.

You have to find a wording of the goal which is satisfactory for the whole team to buy into. It must not look impossible or as though it will fail at the first hurdle. On the other hand it must be stretching enough to be worth the effort which the team is going to put into it.

In terms of measurability, again different teams will be comfortable with different types of goal. They may be quite happy with one which is a measure of quality which they can review and in which they can notice improvement. In which case, the goal will end up something like this:

> *To establish sustainable business relationships with heads of business units, main board directors and IT directors by the end of our next financial year.*

Inside that goal the team then agrees activities which will move it in the direction of the goal. If you like, the measurable part of the goal is contained in the next level of the plan – the activity plan.

Another team will prefer to build into the goal specific actions which will measure whether or not there is an improvement in the information database as a result of raising the level of contact.

In this case the goal would be more like:

> *Within six months to have met with the members of the corporate policy and resources committee and each general manager and financial controller of the four divisions.*
>
> *In each meeting to determine their business goals, strategies and critical success factors.*

Notice how this goal is in two sentences. The plan may look more elegant if each goal is written in one sentence, but elegance is not the point.

The team is trying to agree goals which it will then, over a period of time, try to achieve. If it feels comfortable with what is above then so be it.

Both of these goals do not flawlessly follow the **SMART** template, but both were good enough for a team to change its level of contact dramatically.

Figure 12.1 is an example from the FMCG area followed by the objective

Fig 12.1

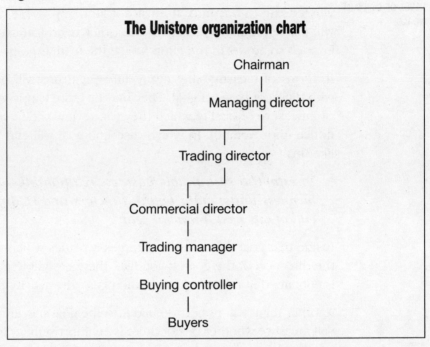

The Unistore organization chart

Chairman
|
Managing director
|
Trading director
|
Commercial director
|
Trading manager
|
Buying controller
|
Buyers

To ensure regular contact at trading director level through meetings with our sales director, with account manager presence at all levels below that. To be achieved within six months.

EXAMPLES OF ACCOUNT PLANNING GOALS

Again, the team has two basic possibilities here. It is probably better if it can agree a long-term goal in this area with a good action plan to demonstrate that it knows how it is going to be achieved. Such a goal would look like this:

Within 18 months to have held a joint planning session with at least two divisional management teams and the corporate policy and resources committee.

The team should remember that it does not have to be a fully-fledged three-day planning session in the first place. It may be more achievable to limit the aspiration to a one-day session where there is a well thought out and agreed agenda, driven by the account team.

It may be more important at this time to concentrate on an internal goal, particularly if the team or the account is new. In this case the team may decide to look at roles and responsibilities internally.

To build a focused global team with defined roles, responsibilities and communications processes in place by the end of the calendar year. To agree these with the appropriate managers prior to the definition of next year's targets.

Pipeline goals tend to be the most quantifiable of the account management goals. After all, basic selling technique tells us to understand what our hit rate is in turning prospects into orders.

We know the order target, either because it is given to us by management or because it is driven by the market share goal. From that and the picture of the current pipeline we can calculate what we have to identify.

You also need to take into account the selling cycle.

You also need to take into account the selling cycle. If it takes on average three months to take an opportunity from discovery to fruition, then that also helps to dictate what amount of pipeline is needed and when.

Calculating the pipeline requirement

Total market next year	£10,000,000
Market share required	25%
Orders needed this year	£2,500,000
Normal hit rate	One success in two campaigns
Pipeline required	£5,000,000
Current pipeline	£1,500,000
Shortfall	£3,500,000

This would lead to a pipeline goal as follows:

By three-quarters of the way through the company year to have identified new potential orders to the value of £3,500,000.

All the sub-account managers would then take their share of this prospecting job in their parts of the account.

In this way the team has addressed the key weakness areas discovered in the environmental analysis.

FURTHER
EXAMPLES OF
ACCOUNT
MANAGEMENT
GOALS

To perform consistently to agreed standards of service, net-work performance and communications (eg every letter answered within 24 hours) by a date agreed with the customer in discussions about the benchmarks for this goal.

Measuring customer satisfaction by criteria agreed specifically with the account itself is always preferable to using generalized customer surveys.

To demonstrate our capability to match our services to the company's business objectives.

A good objective for a team which is going to try to demonstrate a particularly good "fit" between the two companies. International spread is frequently a feature of this sort of strategy.

To achieve year-on-year growth in both revenue and adressable market share.

This objective is more to do with protection from the competition than with the annual sales targets, which will still need to be defined.

Many teams have complained that it is not possible to measure market share in a key account. This is either because there are simply too many units out there to count, or because they claim that no two suppliers are selling into exactly the same "market".

I tend to push back on this by pointing out that it is not a mathematically accurate process. What we need is a rough idea of our share which we can then use subsequently as a base point for measuring the trend.

A case from a business plan rather than an account plan will help to make this clearer as shown on page 191.

To agree the annual sales operating plan, defining revenue and market share aspiration for the next three years.

In this case the team is trying to look ahead and agree with resource managers the longer-term way ahead. If this can be achieved, it means that all its activities can be co-ordinated and things pushed in the same direction.

EXAMPLE

When is world class, world class?

A major utility had set a mission statement which included the words "world class" as a measure of its aspirations. Inside that mission it then established a goal to find, from various sources, the "world class" benchmarks.

A year later it was still debating the definition of world class. It dropped the detail and decided to get a rough measure from statutory bodies and two comparable companies. It stopped arguing the points out to five decimal places and chose some measures.

It quickly became apparent where its major weaknesses lay and it was able to alter the business plan to seek improvements in those areas. If it had continued to search for the detailed and up-to-date benchmarks, it would probably never have made the key decisions on where it should prioritize improvement. ○

Despite this agreement of course, management may still have to make changes in years two and three to allow for change in the environment. However, the team is in a better position if such an agreement can be made.

Sales mangers can be cynical about plans which promise little in the short term but rapid growth in due course. In America it is known as the "hockey stick forecast". Produced as a graph it looks like an ice hockey stick. "Not much now but just wait."

The trouble is that most sales managers have at some point accepted a hockey stick forecast, only to find that when the corner should be approaching and the orders flooding in, the team produces another similar graph. It is always jam tomorrow.

Notice how the objective does not include the product mix or the division between standard and strategic products. In that case these details will be in the milestones of the action plan.

A few final points on goal setting. Keep them simple and few in number. If you do that you stand a reasonable chance of avoiding the major pitfall of planning which is to set up a brilliant plan and then fail to implement it.

> **Keep them simple and few in number.**

The chemistry was all wrong

EXAMPLE

A large group of petrol and chemical companies had problems in a small refinery whose ageing plant made it potentially much less productive than others in the group.

It was felt, however, that with good will from staff unions and management, the production could be sufficient to keep the place alive.

Planning teams spent quite a lot of time going through the creative planning process. The teams went right down to supervisor level and the events had the expected impact of improving morale. Everyone started to believe that it could be done.

Unfortunately time passed and not much really changed. They worked hard to implement the ideas in the plan but cynicism was returning as the fundamental measures of product delivered did not really improve.

The group brought in a new managing director as a last effort to sort out the difficult refinery. He turned it round in nine months.

Asked for the secret he said: "When I got here they had 38 objectives. They were all reasonable and initially had the commitment of the people involved, but 38 objectives was impossible. You cannot get cohesion, and eventually no one gets anything done. I limited the objectives to five. By so doing I lost impetus in some areas, but of course they were not the major concerns.

The point is that I got everyone focused on the critical issues. I even took the key words from each of the objectives and displayed them prominently. This kept people thinking about doing everything in a way that assisted us towards the objectives."

The plan was succesful and the plant survived. ○

Make sure that everyone involved understands the values and strategies assumed in the objectives. A major US bank holds regular one-day sessions to make the values relevant at all levels. The banker then lives those values and measures him or herself against them.

CAMPAIGN GOALS   In addition to the account management goals discussed so far, we must not forget that the team also needs to identify the key sales campaigns it intends to fight in the next relevant time period.

Advice on how to set those goals is in Chapter 5.

setting the strategy for achieving the goals and creating action plans

Some goals need little explanation. They are clear and it is easy for everyone to know what must be done. Others are, by their nature, more difficult and it may be helpful to include a strategy statement between the goal and the activity plans.

EXAMPLES OF STRATEGY STATEMENTS Once again keep it simple. The statement should help anyone who is involved in the goal to know how to behave. Here is an example of a strategy statement inside a market share goal.

> *We shall achieve this market share by emphasizing at all times our dominance in the overall market and our knowledge of hundreds of companies getting benefits out of our products and services.*

It is useful to keep this in the front of the minds of anyone having something to do with the account. Everyone from a senior manager to a maintenance person will be encouraged to talk about other sites and companies that they have seen.

In competitive situations where the customer has been using products from another company, I call this my "Come in out of the cold" strategy.

A customer satisfaction goal could have the following strategy statement:

> *By making contact with all the key people on a daily basis, and answering letters within 24 hours.*

CREATING ACTION PLANS If the team has completed a first class SWOT analysis and followed it up with goals which meet all the criteria of the **SMART** acronym, deciding what to do is often straightforward. Once you know what you are going to try to do, the detailed actions should flow reasonably easily.

The key to good action plans are accountability and timescale. The team must allocate a willing owner to each and every action. The owners will then put a timescale on the action which takes into account other things they have to do.

A frequent problem at this stage is over-commitment. In the enthusiasm of the moment, when the team is starting to see solutions to problems which have been nagging away perhaps for years, team members will agree to do things additional to the tasks they already have in timescales which are not feasible.

Make them take out their diaries and see if the short-term actions will fit into what is probably already a busy schedule. It is much better to lengthen the timescales and achieve them.

If the timescales become so unsatisfactory that they threaten the goals or the mission, then the team is going to have to search for more resource.

It is useful to document the goals and action plans as a form. These forms altogether are actually the plan. The SWOT analysis is back-up material used to ensure that the plan meets the key issues of the account.

○ *Try to set a putative goal for the account you have in mind. Check that it is smart and test it with your team or with the customer.*

FAST TRACK

Goal and action plan

Goal

Strategy statement

Activity	Milestone	Time	Responsibility

13

organization and scheduling

how does your company organize itself to
support key account management profitably?

There are many options for reporting structures, profit
centres, account portfolios and planning timetables.
Picking the right one for your type of product, customer
and company is crucial to supporting the activities of
account teams.

organization and structure

It is not possible to generalize about how a company should organize its account management effort. From experience we can make a number of suggestions which at least raise the issues you need to resolve.

It is most important to bear in mind that management has to find a balance between lack of stability in their organization and an overly rigid adherence to the current structure.

Just as in any form of general management, the winners are the ones who recognize the need for change before they are forced into it by a collapse of revenue or profit for whatever reason.

Taking such a possibility into consideration has to be part of an account manager's philosophy. Nothing is permanent.

> **The winners are the ones who recognize the need for change.**

EXAMPLE

If you have to change markets, do it in time

Two independent consultants, previously colleagues in a larger company, had made a decent living out of working in the computer industry for a variety of clients.

In the late '80s they were discussing the problems of the established computer majors and swapping stories about the statements of senior people in the computer world they had spoken to recently.

In piecing it all together, an alarming picture arose. It became clear that everyone was predicting disaster for everyone except themselves. No-one escaped. If company A said that company B was failing to adapt to the new situation, then you could be sure that company C was saying the same of company A and so on.

The consultants mused whether or not the prognostications were true or not. (In the grand majority of cases they were true.)

The two colleagues decided it would be imprudent to do nothing in the face of such evidence. They gave each other the target of getting at least one new client each in a different industry. They chose the telecommunications sector which was in a phase of rapid growth.

Scared of losing face by failing to keep their side of the bargain, the consultants put together sales campaigns and duly delivered one new client each.

Two years later, their businesses were dominated by the telecommunications which was producing more than 80 per cent of their revenues.

Meanwhile the computer industry had gone into total disarray, and the consultancy field was flooded with hundreds of new independents who had been released from the computer industry under the newly-coined euphemism "downsizing". ○

This lack of permanence is true of any account management organization. What works now may not do so well when the company has more accounts, or the market changes.

Against this requirement for flexibility is the opposing need for allowing a structure time to prove itself. Digging up the carrots to see how the roots are doing can upset and demotivate account teams. Continuous change makes the teams wonder if the senior management is in control or has a strategy at all.

I will take the issues for deliberation as follows:

● **Profit centre management.**

● **Reporting structures.**

● **Number of accounts in a territory.**

PROFIT CENTRE MANAGEMENT

I think the case is now proved that a salesperson makes a poor profit centre. If you give a salesperson the automatic right, for example, to offer a 10 per cent discount he or she will tend to make the concession too early in the sales process. In fact, salespeople have a tendency to give their best shot on price the moment the customer suggests they may have a price disadvantage.

In my opinion a salesperson should be encouraged to seek volume, to sell as high a value of product as possible at the price on the price list. If they know what the transfer prices are they will berate management for concessions down to a price which is easier for them to sell at.

On a need to know basis, then, the salesperson can operate quite happily with a hazy idea of the margins and costs of selling which management are working with.

In account management the situation can be very different. Particularly in the case of a key account manager who has other salespeople taking the orders in the account, it may be advisable to organize the account as a profit centre.

At least account managers' profit and loss accounts should show the transfer price or gross margin as well as the costs of the resources deployed on the account.

If it is a worldwide account this can be difficult to organize from a management information point of view. However, it is not good enough to put this up as an excuse if the profit and loss account is the right way to go.

A profit centre is truly a profit centre when the manager is given the responsibility of the asset base he or she is using to make money. I have seen only failed attempts to put asset management down to first line management. If you ask account managers to look after the company's assets it tends to take their eye off the customer orientation.

EXAMPLE

Finance pressure can become counter productive

I worked with a company which, because it had got itself into serious financial problems, recruited a new managing director whose background was finance.

He rightly diagnosed the root of the problem as being in sales management. The sales managers were used to working with high gross margins and had developed expensive habits of discounting and providing free support.

They were not "spending the company's money as though it were their own" and the company had become vulnerable to any slow down of revenue which threatened to cause further cash problems.

By Herculean effort the company's accountants produced the information

> **He rightly diagnosed the root of the problem as being in sales management.**

and systems to push real profit centre management down to first line sales managers.

This lasted only for one year. The sales managers became totally introverted about their p and l's and balance sheets. If, for example, a salesperson wanted to offer a trade-in of an old product to support a campaign to sell a new one, sales managers would spend a huge effort to unload the second-hand product on someone else's territory. If they failed to do so, the product was charged to their profit and loss account.

They would disallow sales in favour of making money in some other way.

It cannot be said that the year-long experiment did not work. Once the situation was made more standard by lifting the level of profit centres, the first line managers were much more conscious of selling profitably. ○

I believe that salespeople should report to sales managers. This means that where a key account manager has sub-accountees selling for him or her in different locations, there is only charismatic power and leadership available to the account manager.

This will only work if the planning regime is tight and sales managers have signed off on the amount of time their salespeople will work on the various accounts.

There is a supply and demand situation here. If it is easier to make sales target from customers who are not in a particular key account, then that is what salespeople will do. It is up to the account manager to produce an account environment which enables the sub-accountees to sell more easily to their customers.

The same is true for support and maintenance management. However, where there is a considerable amount of, for example, technical support involved in every sale then there is an important decision to be made. At what level do the sales and support organizations come under the same manager? It is almost certain that it should be well below the managing director.

The most successful organizations I have seen have had support managers reporting into sales at second or even first line management. You need an audit function of course, with senior support people in staff jobs with a remit to ensure the integrity of what the support people under sales management are doing.

○ *Consider what your profit centres and reporting structures are at present, and write down the arguments for change.*

○ *Remember that whatever your answer to these questions is right now, you will have to review it in the not too distant future.*

FAST TRACK

**NUMBER OF
ACCOUNTS IN A
TERRITORY**

If you are looking after companies which are in the top 500 in size, then you have to be practical about your workload. If you consider the amount of effort required to carry out all the professional processes in this book and then keep the plans up to date, you can see that in all probability only one can receive this full treatment.

If you only have one account then there is no problem. Carry out the processes on the parts of the customer where there is current or potential return.

If you have more than one account, you need to pick one out for the full treatment and then look for practical short cuts for the others.

In the next part of this chapter, I will make a suggestion as to what these short cuts may be.

THE ANNUAL PLANNING TIMETABLE

For a key account to prosper, there needs to be an annual schedule of planning and forecasting activity. The following table is an example which you will need to modify to reflect your mix of accounts

In the table, the month refers to the month in the supplying company's financial year.

I have assumed as a starting point that before the first event, the team has updated its database of knowledge in the account. The team members understand the structure and know the key people they need to work with.

The team further understands the financial position of the client and its goals and critical success factors. As has been said before, if this database of knowledge is poor then the first planning session will be short and simply allocate tasks to the team to plug the knowledge gap.

I have also assumed that marketing strategies and other internal essential knowledge is available to the team.

The length of the events are drawn from experience, but you will have to check their validity in your environment.

Event	Document	Month	Comments
Annual planning event (3 days)	First draft of updated account plan. Includes a list of the likely key campaign plans	9	This event may or may not include the customer for, say, day one. If the customer attends more than the first day the team may have to get together again to complete the more confidential part of the plan. ▶

2 1 2 an an annn an naan ana

Event	Document	Month	Comments
			It is likely that the team will present the draft to a senior manager to ensure that its aspirations are consistent with the selling company's strategies, particularly on resources
C-SWOT validation	Updated account plan	10	The account manager will hold a series of meetings with the customer to validate and improve the C-SWOT. I have assumed that it is not necessary to get the team together again to update the plan
Campaign planning	Campaign plans or updates of existing ones	10	Produces plans for the key campaigns highlighted in the account plan
Preparation of annual sales operating plan	Sales forecast. Resource requirements. Input to marketing	11	This shows the forecast for revenue and orders in detail for the next company year, and in outline for two further years.
			It also has the resource requirements for the account management objectives as well as the campaign plan activities.
			The resource requirements will include the need for senior managers to make sales calls in the account.
Annual management review	Agreement to the resources requested or instructions to think again	12 or 1 in next year	NB Make sure that everybody knows that this is a decision-making forum. If, on the other hand, management is not in a position to allocate resources this must be made clear to everyone
Account team review (2 days)	Updates of account and campaign plans	3	An important review since it is not too late to make changes to ensure a successful year.
Account team review (1 day)	Updated account and campaign plans	6	

Note that this table is for a key account manager. If there are more than one of these on the account you will have to organize the sub-account planning session to coincide with or be compatible with this top level of planning.

> **It is likely that the team will present the draft to a senior manager.**

For the shortened version the account manager would do those parts concerned with campaign plans and the annual sales operating plan. The resource requirement would in that case only come from the campaign plans.

Creating a new plan or the annual planning review

Session: An initial meeting to create a new plan or complete a major annual review.

Delegates:

1. The worldwide team brought together for the annual event.

2. Marketing representatives.

3. The customer for the customer environmental analysis.

Objective: To produce the best possible plan to attain a mission statement or achieve an objective.

Timescale: Three days.

Timetable Day 1

9.00   Introduction to the planning process by the facilitator and team agreement to the process and disciplines.

9.40   Agreement to the S-Mission Statement or the Objective which acts as the scope of the planning session.

10.00   Definition of the C-Mission.

10.30   Coffee.

10.45   C-SWOT analysis to identify the strengths and weaknesses of the customer in striving to achieve the C-Mission.

12.30 Lunch.

1.30 C-SWOT analysis (continued).

3.30 Coffee.

3.45 Start of S-SWOT to identify the supplying company's strengths and weaknesses in striving to achieve the S-Mission.

5.30 End of session.

Timetable Day 2

9.00 S-SWOT (continued).

10.30 Coffee.

11.45 S-SWOT (continued).

12.30 Lunch.

1.30 S-SWOT (continued).

3.30 Coffee.

3.45 Facilitator presents and presides over the C-SWOT to S-SWOT check and the creation of the control matrix and spider's web.

4.30 Facilitator presents rules for setting SMART goals and action plans with accountability.

4.45 Goal setting, account management goals.

6.30 End of session.

Timetable Day 3

9.00 Goal setting, account management goals (continued) and campaign goals.

10.30 Coffee.

10.45 Goal setting (continued).

11.45 Split into relevant teams to plan activities.

12.30 Lunch.

1.30   Activity planning.

3.30   Coffee.

3.45   Activity planning (continued).

5.00   Presentation to senior manager of the plan so far.

6.30   End of session.

Once an account team has produced an account plan and agreed with senior management that it should be implemented, the reviewing of that plan is strongly analogous to a Board of Directors' meeting.

> **The reviewing of that plan is strongly analogous to a Board of Directors' meeting.**

Such a team must meet monthly or quarterly to agree progress on the plan, take remedial action where required and then consider the longer-term issues which may alter current strategy or offer new opportunities.

The objective is to amend the plan in accordance with achievements to date and changes in the environment.

The review process

Timescale: Maximum 1 day.

Agenda

Prior to the meeting, each "owner" of a goal should submit to the administrator a note of progress towards their account management and campaign goals. These should be circulated along with a statement of the issues to be discussed in the afternoon session.

Morning: Each campaign goal "owner" should briefly introduce progress to date and suggest amendments.

The account team discusses and agrees changes to the plan, particularly agreeing new actions to overcome obstacles which are proving difficult to remove.

Afternoon: The afternoon is kept for longer-term issues. It is vital that the operational problems discussed in the morning session do not overflow into the afternoon and stop the "Board" from assessing new opportunities and looking ahead.

The team should consider:

1. Amendments to the associated SWOT analysis.

2. Issues requiring remedial actions.

3. Recommendations for decisions.

The facilitator is a useful person in such a meeting and has a role very similar to a non-executive director. Where the account team, for example, might duck an issue which is difficult to resolve the facilitator will intervene. The facilitator is important in maintaining good planning disciplines.

Some issues in the afternoon session may be large enough to require the statement of a mission or aiming focus, followed by a SWOT analysis and the setting of goals and action plans in the usual way.

At this stage, the team may realize that the problem or opportunity under discussion needs more time or a different natural planning team. In this case the action plan will be to hold a planning session for the appropriate people at a suitable time.

It is at the afternoon session that the team could invite other speakers to make presentations on new or changing parts of the business environment.

○ *Draw up a suitable timetable for your key account plan and campaign plans.*

FAST TRACK

appendix 1

---

campaign planner

summary sheet and forms

Use these forms to document the campaign planning process. If your team has access to computers, it is useful to put these forms into a computer file.

Summary sheet

- **What is the campaign goal?**

  _____

  _____

- **What are the real business benefits?**

  _____

  _____

- **How well is the project qualified?**

  _____

  _____

- **Who are the key buyers?**

  _____

  _____

- **What power and influence is exerted?**

  _____

  _____

- **Where do they stand?**

  _____

  _____

- **How receptive are they to change?**

  _____

  _____

- **Who will drive and who will restrain?**

  _____

  _____

What is the campaign goal?

(**S**tretching, **m**easurable, **a**chievable, related to the customer, **t**ime targeted)

● **What is the customer's business objective for this campaign?**

_____

_____

_____

_____

● **What critical success factors declared by the customer does this campaign address?**

_____

_____

_____

_____

● **What benefits both tangible and intangible will the customer derive from a successful implementation?**

_____

_____

_____

_____

● **What are the rough costs of all the expenditure involved?**

_____

_____

_____

_____

- How does the *prima facie* return on investment case look?

  _____

  _____

  _____

  _____

- What key ratios will be the basis of how the customer measures the success of the project?

  _____

  _____

  _____

  _____

- Where in terms of geography and company divisions will the benefits occur?

  _____

  _____

  _____

  _____

- What are the risks which the customer will take if they go ahead with this project?

  _____

  _____

  _____

  _____

- How does the size of this project compare with others the customer has undertaken?

  _____

  _____

  _____

  _____

How well is the campaign qualified?

To assess qualification use the following convention:

✓ means there is no more work to be done in this area.

? means that there is some work to be done or that we are not sure of the situation.

✗ means that there is a lot of work to be done or we have a problem.

Qualification questions	✓/?/✗	Which key person do we talk to?
Customer need Is it a real need? Is the requirement strategic to the customer? Is the campaign worth the necessary effort?		
Finance Is the money available in a budget? Do all the key people have a rough cost expectation? Is the necessary return on investment process done?		
Key people Do we know all the key people? Do we have the same access to key people as our competitors? Are they all informed of the pending buying decision?		

Qualification questions	✓ / ? / X	Which key person do we talk to?
Timescale Have the key people agreed on a decision date? Is there an agreed implementation timescale?		
Solution Is our solution valid? Is the risk of our being able to deliver promises acceptable? Is the project profitable now or through future sales?		
Basis of decision Have we agreed with the key people their criteria for going ahead? Have we influenced this?		
Implementability Are the customer's implementation resources available and allocated to this project? Do we have management agreement to the necessary sales resources? Are the implementation resources from our side identified and allocated?		
Competitive position Can we identify one or more areas where we have competitive advantage? Is there an acceptably small number of competitors bidding?		

Qualification spider's web

Fig A1.1

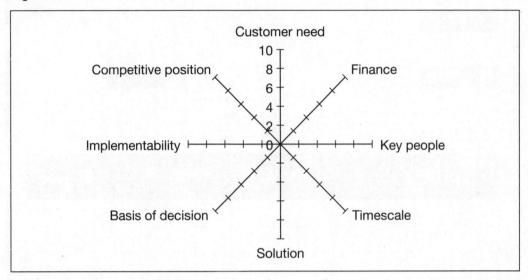

It is useful to put this into a spreadsheet.

Activity sheet

COMPANY

CAMPAIGN

PERSON(S)

ACTIVITY	OBJECTIVE	WHEN	WHO

Account management spider's web

Fig A1.2

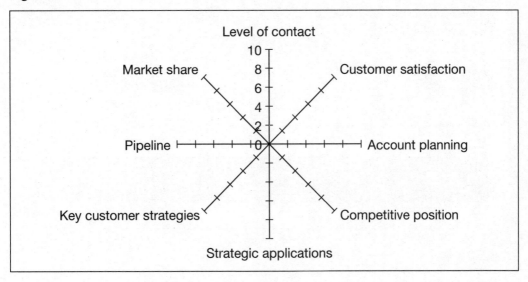

appendix 2

---

investment appraisal

a short introduction to cost benefit analysis

If account managers are to put themselves properly into the shoes of the customer, they need to understand the basics of how managers and accountants go about cost justification.

the process of cost justification

The cost justification process can be described under five headings:

- Choose a timescale.

- Estimate the costs of the project capital and revenue (running).

- Agree an estimate of the benefits.

- Analyze the project for risk and adjust the cost justification accordingly.

The second part of this appendix looks at the accountancy techniques used to compare one project with another. The aim of this is to give the Board the financial information it needs to decide where to put its available funds.

CHOOSE A TIMESCALE

There is frequently a company norm for investment appraisal which covers the timescale. Many computer projects are measured over five years, projects concerning vehicles over three and so on. In FMCG the timescales of market testing for example could be much shorter.

At the other end of the spectrum digging a tunnel under the English Channel and providing a transport system to the rest of the continent of Europe probably needs to be examined over tens of years.

The timescale is often impacted by the finance department's policy on the depreciation of fixed assets. The key thing is to choose a time period which is appropriate to what is physically going to happen.

EXAMPLE

Testing the viability of a telephone opportunity

After cable TV had been introduced in the UK, the time came for the successful cable companies to examine the case for adding telephony to their service portfolios.

It is technically a relatively straightforward process to add the telephony dimension when a cable TV company has gone through the capital consuming business of laying cable past a significant number of houses and businesses in the area.

▶

There were two parameters set by management as the financial basis of decision. The telephony project would not be allowed to delay the break-even point of the TV business. Break-even occurred on the original project at 10 years, so that became, *ipso facto*, the timescale for telephony.

The second parameter was that the telephony project should not delay the time at which the TV project produced a positive annual cashflow. This further defined timescale as the TV showed a positive cashflow in year six. ○

Some management teams are better than others at accepting long-term commitments of cash to projects which take time to get started. Indeed it has been said that the dominance of American companies in the UK cable TV industry was caused by British management teams being uncomfortable with such lengthy break-even periods.

The timescale is often impacted by the finance department's policy on the depreciation of fixed assets.

Again the account manager's participation in the timescale choice can be crucial. Who else knows better how projects pan out than the supplier who has been involved before?

ESTIMATE THE COSTS OF THE PROJECT BOTH CAPITAL AND REVENUE (RUNNING)

Because it is relatively simple to make sure that good estimates of cost are made, this part of the investment appraisal process is usually done comprehensively.

The job of the professional account manager is to make sure that all the costs are taken into account at the earliest possible stage. Competitive edge can be won if you are the person who reminds prospects that there will be running costs that they have ignored.

The job of the professional account manager is to make sure that all the costs are taken into account at the earliest possible stage.

Competitive edge can certainly be lost if the opposite occurs and prospects have these extra costs brought to their attention by someone else.

A comprehensive cost list

The costings checklist for selling the Dialcard product looks like this:

- Staff time for evaluation.
- Production of unique numbering system.
- Logo design for the front and back sides of the card.
- Printing of letters and other matter to be sent out with the Dialcard.
- Automatic insertion of the Dialcard into envelopes.
- Postage.
- Helping desk resources for customer queries.
- Amendment of computer system to recognize the Dialcard and its access numbers.
- Running costs of the amended computer system.
- Advertising costs.

The salesperson for Dialcard will introduce all of these costs at an early stage. It proves his professionalism and at worst gives early warning that the customer is going to reject the project on the grounds of cost. It is poor practice to allow these costs to leak out as the evaluation is made.

Publishing company chooses telephone system

Royston Publishing Ltd is examining the opportunity to buy a new telephone switch-board and associated equipment. The additional costs are calculated as follows:

- Capital expenditure £600,000.
- Annual maintenance £60,000.
- Annual telephone network additional charges £100,000.

AGREE AN ESTIMATE OF THE BENEFITS

This is normally the most tricky part of the cost justification process. It involves managers making estimates of what will happen in the future and then taking responsibility for achieving those results.

It also includes the agreeing of benefits which are hard to turn into tangible or measurable ones. Persuading managers to accept that the results of investment can be measured deserves attention from an account manager. In this way he or she starts to understand how the benefits of his or her products and services come through.

EXAMPLE

Following the example above, the benefits to Royston Publishing Ltd of its new equipment are calculated as follows:

Tangible benefits		Intangible benefits	
Reduce exchange lines	£12,000	Increase advertising	£338,885
Reduce direct lines	£24,000	Reduce interest on overdraft	£239,500
Reduce call charges	£180,000	Reduced staff turnover	£300,000
Reduce operators	£120,000	**Total**	**£878,385**
Reduce space	£39,000		
Reduce courier charges	£36,000		
Total	**£411,000**		

ANALYZE THE PROJECT FOR RISK AND ADJUST THE COST JUSTIFICATION ACCORDINGLY

There is only one certainty when managers make estimates of costs and benefits, and that is that they will be wrong. In the decision-making process it is important therefore to analyze the comparative risk of one project with another.

In the case of costs it is relatively simple to make an allowance for contingency, often a simple percentage of the likely costs.

It should be understood that the mean or most likely outcome is the one which managers are expecting to deliver and the major judgement on the project will be decided on that. However, it can easily change financial priorities if a risky project with a relatively high return is compared with one with a lower return and more certainty of outcome.

> **Make an allowance for contingency, often a simple percentage of the likely costs.**

Here is the Royston case with attention paid to the manager's view on risk. Where he has given an estimate on which he is entirely comfortable that value has gone into the pessimistic column. Where he has stated a possibility if all goes really well it is the value used in the optimistic column. The mean column represents his best shot at what will actually happen.

The costs have been accepted as including some contingency.

Tangible benefits	Optimistic £	Mean £	Pessimistic £
Reduce exchange lines	15,000	12,000	9,000
Reduce direct lines	30,000	24,000	18,000
Reduce call charges	210,000	180,000	150,000
Reduce operators	150,000	120,000	90,000
Reduce space	39,000	39,000	39,000
Reduce courier charges	42,000	36,000	30,000
Total	**£486,000**	**£411,000**	**£336,000**
Intangible benefits			
Increase advertising	677,770	338,885	169,442
Reduce interest on overdraft	424,400	239,500	54,600
Reduced staff turnover	375,000	300,000	225,000
Total	**£1,477,170**	**£878,385**	**£449,042**

Tangible benefits	Optimistic £	Mean £	Pessimistic £
Reduce exchange lines	15,000	12,000	9,000
Reduce direct lines	30,000	24,000	18,000
Reduce call charges	210,000	180,000	150,000
Reduce operators	150,000	120,000	90,000
Reduce space	39,000	39,000	39,000
Reduce courier charges	42,000	36,000	30,000
Total	**£486,000**	**£411,000**	**£336,000**
Costs			
Annual maintenance	60,000	60,000	60,000
Additional operator charges	100,000	100,000	100,000
Net saving	**£326,000**	**£251,000**	**£170,000**
Capital expenditure	**£600,000**	**£600,000**	**£600,000**
Payback period	**1.8 years**	**2.4 years**	**3.4 years**

USE ACCOUNTANCY
TECHNIQUES TO
COMPARE THIS
PROJECT WITH
OTHER USES TO
WHICH THE FUNDS
COULD BE PUT
To complete the Royston case the above table shows a simple payback calculation assuming that the Board has insisted that payback should be within two years.

Notice how the intangible benefits are absent. It is usual to test the outcome without the intangibles first, and only rely on them if the tangibles are not sufficient.

This is very useful information as a basis for a management decision. It is clear that the pessimistic benefits case would not be sufficient to meet the two year payback criteria.

If Royston decides to go ahead with the project the managers will pay special attention to achieving the mean estimate of benefits.

So far we have only looked at the payback method of investment appraisal. This simply looks at the length of time it takes for the project's costs and benefits to break even and management prefer the shortest project.

This is reasonable in many ways. It has the advantage of being straightforward and easy to calculate and explain. It suffers from the problem that it takes no account of projects whose benefits improve in the longer term.

Thus management will always err to projects with fast payback. Once again this is not unreasonable since if you get investment money back quickly you can always use it to reinvest in something else.

However, superior methods of investment appraisal exist and are in frequent use. The one which current wisdom suggests is the most helpful in decision-making because of its accurate measure of time as well as value is the discounted cashflow.

investment appraisal techniques

**METHODS OF
INVESTMENT
APPRAISAL**
The most common methods of appraising projects are as follows:

- **Return on capital employed.**

- **Payback period.**

- **Discounted cashflow.**

Return on Capital Employed (RoCE) Here is an example of a management team evaluating a project using this method:

Costs and benefits	Amount
Asset costs	£10,000
Estimated value at end of project	Nil
Expected earnings (before depreciation)	
Year 1	£2,000
Year 2	£ 3,000
Year 3	£ 5,000
Year 4	£ 7,000
Year 5	£ 8,000
Total	**£25,000**
Net earnings over 5 years	£15,000
Average earnings	£3,000
Average return on capital employed	**30% (3,000/10,000)**

It is sometimes argued that the average capital employed of £5,000 should be used instead of £10,000. On this basis, the answer to the previous example would be 60%. Either method can be employed as long as this is done consistently.

RoCE has the disadvantage that it does not take into account the time when the return is received. Thus it is possible to have two projects having the same RoCE but one project starts immediately and the other has a pre-production period of say, two years.

> **RoCE has the disadvantage that it does not take into account the time when the return is received.**

Payback period This method measures the length of time from the first payment of cash until the total receipts of cash from the investment equals the total payment made on that investment. It does not in any way attempt to measure the profitability of the project and restricts all calculations to a receipts and payments basis.

In considering alternative projects, it is the one with the shortest pay-back period which management prefer. Here is an example:

	Project 1	Project 2
Asset cost	£10,000	£15,000
Net cashflow		
Year 1	£2,000	£3,000
Year 2	£3,000	£4,000
Year 3	£3,000	£6,000
Year 4	£4,000	£8,000
Year 5	£2,000	£8,000
Payback period	**3.5 years**	**3.25 years**

The payback period method has two major disadvantages:

1. It considers only cash received during the payback period and does not take into account anything received afterwards.

2. It does not take into account the dates on which the cash is actually received. Thus it is possible to have two projects both costing the same, with the same payback period, but with different cashflows:

	Project 1	Project 2
Asset cost	£10,000	£10,000
Net cashflow		
Year 1	£1,000	£3,000
Year 2	£3,000	£3,000
Year 3	£3,000	£3,000
Year 4	£3,000	£1,000
Year 5	£4,000	£4,000
Payback period	**4 years**	**4 years**

Although both projects have the same payback period, most people would prefer Project 2, as the cash is received earlier, and thus it can be reinvested to earn more profits.

The technique used to allow for the timings of the cashflow is known as discounted cashflow.

This method works on the basis that an individual would be prepared to exchange an amount of money due today for a higher amount due sometime in the future.

Therefore cashflows due in the future may be converted to equally desirable cashflows due today. The way that is done is by discounting the cash due in future years.

Here is an example of a discounted cashflow:

Timing of cashflow	Amount of cashflow	Discount factor at 10%	Present value
Immediate	(£10,000)	1	(£10,000)
After year 1	£3,000	0.909	£2,727
After year 2	£4,000	0.826	£3,304
After year 3	£5,000	0.751	£3,755
After year 4	£3,000	0.683	£2,049

The usefulness of this example is that it has reduced all the numbers to comparability. By discounting the cashflows you can calculate the net present value by totalling the figures in the last column.

In this case the net present value (NPV) is £1,835 positive. This means that the project does pass the test of a rate of return of 10%.

1. For convenience, timing is considered to start at time 0 and future cashflows occur on the anniversary of the initial investment. This usually has the effect of delaying income and making a project appear less desirable.

To overcome this, cashflows may be allocated to shorter periods (eg quarters) and the appropriate discount factors used.

2. Cashflows must be relevant costs and benefits. (See below)

3. The discount rate represents the cost of capital. In a large company this will be laid down by the treasury function and is linked to actual interest rates.

4. Projects with a positive net present value make a positive contribution to the value of the company and should be accepted.

Developments of the basic problem

Internal rate of return

This is the discounting rate which when applied to the cashflows gives a net present value of zero. Whilst it is commonly used in practice it is theoretically inferior to NPV for three reasons:

- **IRR would prefer a return of 30% on an investment of £2,000 to a return of 28% on £3 million (The problem of scale).**

- **IRR assumes reinvestment of surplus funds is possible at the IRR. This can be very inaccurate.**

- **In some circumstances there may be more than one IRR for a project or there may be no IRR**

IRR can be computed by trial and error or more conveniently by using an appropriate computer package (eg Lotus 1-2-3).

The incremental method

Where two projects are mutually exclusive (eg the lease-buy decision) they may be compared by looking at the differences between them and therefore cashflows which occur under either option are omitted.

Inflation

The discount rate is usually quoted at the market rate which includes an allowance for inflation. Cashflows should therefore be estimated at the amount that will actually arise in the future.

An alternative approach involves stating all cashflows at their current value and discounting using a (hypothetical) real rate. This approach is not recommended since it is difficult to use when inflation rates vary between different elements of cost.

Tax

The tax effect of a project should be based on the change in profit as a result of the project. Remember to remove depreciation from the calculation and replace it with capital allowances. Tax is usually payable/recoverable nine months after the year to which it relates.

Risk

There are many methods employed in practice to consider risk. These include:

Sensitivity analysis: What is the effect on NPV of changes in inputs? How far can inputs change before the project becomes undesirable?

Expected value analysis: Each variable is given a range of values with associated probabilities. These are then dealt with either by calculating average NPV (the expected value) or by computing an optimistic, pessimistic and most likely result.

Risk matrix: Benefits are ranked according to how likely they are to arise. The analysis then involves including these in the computation in order of likelihood until costs are covered.

The appraisal of any proposed project must be performed on the basis of **relevant** costs and revenues. A cost (or revenue) is relevant to a decision if the cost changes as a result of that decision.

Be careful that your assumptions are checked out by someone who is qualified to distinguish relevant from irrelevant. Whether you like it or not, there are accountancy techniques *in play* here and common sense does not always give you the correct answer.

THE RELEVANCE OF COSTS AND BENEFITS

The following classification of costs is useful in this respect.

Fixed and variable costs

How do costs react to changes in activity level, for example higher sales? Fixed costs are constant in total throughout a relevant range. Variable costs are constant per unit of output.

Direct and indirect costs

Direct costs are those that may be directly attributed to a cost unit (eg a product or department). Indirect costs are those that are apportioned between cost units on some reasonable basis. It should be noted that a cost may be direct with respect to one cost unit and indirect with respect to another.

Avoidable and unavoidable costs   Can a cost be avoided by making a particular decision? The commonest example of an unavoidable cost is a cost that has already been incurred and cannot now be altered. Such costs are called **sunk costs**.

These classifications may be applied to the costs faced by a company to help in establishing whether a cost is relevant to a decision or not.

Material   The quantity of material used will normally depend on production. If this is the case then the material is known as direct material. Direct material will be a variable cost if the cost per unit of material does not change. Changes may be caused by price rises/reductions or quantity discounts.

If material is in stock already, then the original purchase price is a sunk cost and therefore irrelevant. The relevant cost of the material is its value to the business and can be obtained by answering the question "what will we do with this material if we do not use it in the proposed contract?"

Labour   Labour involved in production rather than supervision is known as direct labour. The cost of direct labour is usually considered to be a variable cost.

The relevant cost of labour for a contract depends on whether the contract can be met by the existing workforce in normal hours or whether it is necessary to recruit, work overtime or give up other profitable projects.

Overheads   Overheads must be classified into those that change with output (variable) and those that are fixed. Fixed overheads are irrelevant to a decision unless incremental fixed overheads are incurred

Fixed assets   The cost of new assets is usually easy to establish. Assets already owned are subject to the same test as materials in stock. It will be the cash paid or income foregone which is the relevant cost of an asset. Existing book value and depreciation are always irrelevant to a decision.

Having established the amount and timing of relevant costs and revenues these may be used in some method of investment appraisal.

index

The text contains a number of case histories and examples. These are identified individually in the index, either by company name or by company business.

Other titles in this series

creating buyer relationships

Daragh O' Reilly & Julian J Gibas

Within business-to-business markets the skill and professionalism of the buyer is continuously improving. The result of this is that the marketer is in danger of being left behind, which makes the sales and marketing effort ever more difficult.

The only way to rise to this challenge is to radically reappraise the management of your buyer relationships. Based on the latest thinking in marketing and right up-to-date sales practice, this book strips away the mystery and complexity of business-to-business marketing.

If you think you need more leverage when dealing with professional buyers this book wil tell you how to get it.

ISBN 0273 61692 7   Price £19.99

direct hit – direct marketing

Merlin Stone, Derek Davies & Alison Bond

Direct Marketing is an essential part of marketing. Any company that ignores direct marketing does so at its peril. It enables you to communicate with your customers to let them know you are there, ensure that your products fulfil their needs, receive valuable feedback, build up a database and develop long-term loyalty.

This book is a no-nonsense practical tool kit which will enable you to launch a successful direct marketing campaign. It is essential reading for all organizations, in all industries, whatever their size.

ISBN 0273 61689 7   Price £19.99

Other titles in this series

customer focused marketing plans

Angela Hatton

The consultant challenge every manager today faces is to put the customer at the heart of their business, whilst getting "more from less" resources. The key to success lies in planning. Not the routine annual ritual of preparing documents which gather dust all year. Rather planning as a dynamic and continuous management activity. Plans which are easy to produce and practical to use.

This book presents you with a fresh insight into the value of planning. Not a theoretical thesis, it's a hands-on planning made simple, but effective approach.

ISBN 0273 61693 5   Price £19.99

database marketing

Ian Linton

Have you ever wondered how Virgin knows which paper you like to read and have it ready on your seat when you board your flight? Or how on earth can Marriot hotels keep track of the likes and dislikes of 5 million people, even down to their favourite room? Are these people psychics?

No, but they have learnt how powerful a marketing tool a database can be. Are you getting the most out of your database? This book shows you how to use the information you have to improve your performance and customer relations. if you want to have spot on marketing, which will wow your customers, this book will give you the know-how you need.

ISBN 0273 61179 8   Price £19.99

Please note that all prices are subject to change.